Anguel S. Stefanov

Space and Time

Philosophical Problems

MINKOWSKI
Institute Press

Anguel S. Stefanov
Institute of Philosophy and Sociology
at the Bulgarian Academy of Sciences
angstefanov@abv.bg

Cover: God Janus (image taken from https://www.sonjaweilenmann.ch/2016/01/08/januar/?print=print)

ISBN: 978-1-927763-82-7 (softcover)
ISBN: 978-1-927763-83-4 (ebook)

Minkowski Institute Press
Montreal, Quebec, Canada
http://minkowskiinstitute.org/mip/

For information on all Minkowski Institute Press publications visit
our website at http://minkowskiinstitute.org/mip/books/

CONTENTS

1 Introduction   **1**

2 **Do Space and Time Exist?**   **5**
   2.1 The Common View of Space and Time   5
   2.2 From a Physical Point of View   7
   2.3 From a Logical and Ontological Point of View   12

3 **Transcendental Philosophy about Space and Time**   **17**
   3.1 The neglected alternative   18
   3.2 The phenomenological character of the common concepts of space and time   23

4 **A-Theory and B-Theory of Time: Is There Middle Way?**   **27**
   4.1 The Controversy among Theorists of Time   27
   4.2 Baker's View   30
   4.3 The Deficiency of Baker's BA-Theory of Time   32
   4.4 Attempt at an Elaboration of Baker's BA-Theory of Time   34

5 **The Growing Block Theory**   **47**

6 **The Phenomenology of Temporal Passage**   **55**
   6.1 Preliminary Words about the Mind-Dependence of Temporal Passage   55
   6.2 The Moving Spotlight Theories   56
   6.3 The Mind-Dependence of the Passage of Time   65

7 **Does Time Flow, at any Rate?**   **73**

8 The Relationalist-Substantivalist Debate **91**
8.1 Preliminary Words 91
8.2 Leibniz's Shift Argument Revisited. The Void Argument 92
8.3 Properties of Spacetime as an Entity 96
8.4 Argument from a Consistent Interpretation of the Basic Equation in General Relativity 99

9 Time Travel **103**
9.1 Introductory Words 103
9.2 Curious Facts Concerning Time Travel 104
9.3 Ontological and Logical Constraints to Time Travel . 105
9.4 My Thesis 111

10 Conclusion **119**

A Zeno's Paradoxes and the Failure of Their Alleged Solutions Based on the Common View of Space and Time **123**

B The Arrow of Time and Irreversible Processes **133**

References **138**

1 INTRODUCTION

This book is comprised of interconnected philosophical analyses of conceptions of space, time, and spacetime. Trivial as it may seem, but I have to say something at the very outset, though briefly, why I propose such a book to the reading public. I have to do so, at least because of the fact that a good deal of impressive philosophical work has been published since ancient times till present day about grasping the nature of space and time. So, why another work ought to appear on this topic?

I can certainly point out that this topic is fundamental for philosophy, as well as for physics and cosmology. But, no less certainly, this circumstance does not seem to give enough reason for someone to embark on such an enterprise, aiming merely at presenting yet another story about space and time (usually based on retelling old stories). Thus there must be another justification for my attempt. And it may be only one. It is the proviso that a book suggests more or less sound arguments in favour of definite, out of different combatting positions concerning the understanding of space and time; and even more, suggests some original view to be defended within the ongoing debates about the nature of spacetime. My humble effort here is made for the sake of such an expectation.

The understanding of space and time is confronted with a large field of controversies with many intertwined *lines of debate*. To mention just a few: whether space and time have an independent existence of matter, whether they exist independently of one another, whether they exist independently of the mind, what is their nature – relational or substantive, what accounts for the so called time arrow(s), whether times other than the present moment exist, and if so, how they exist, does time really flow, as well as many

1

other specifying issues along each of the lines of debate.

As Brian Greene puts it at the very beginning of his voluminous book *"The Fabric of the Cosmos"* (2004: IX):

> Space and time capture the imagination like no other scientific subject. For good reason. They form the arena of reality, the very fabric of the cosmos. Our entire existence – everything we do, think, and experience – takes place in some region of space during some interval of time. Yet science is still struggling to understand what space and time actually are. Are they real physical entities or simply useful ideas?

Even this short frank avowal to the effect that "science is still struggling to understand what space and time actually are" bears a deep philosophical problem: the one about the way of existence of space and time. From one side it is contended that "they form the arena of reality, the very fabric of the cosmos", while from another side B. Greene expresses a doubt whether they are "real physical entities or simply useful ideas". If space and time are taken to be simply useful ideas without any real referent, they could hardly be accepted to form the very fabric of the cosmos.

In this book I shall make an attempt at raising arguments *pro and con* the confronting positions along some of the here mentioned lines of debate. In so doing I shall not put a basic accent on the historical context of the debates, but rather on the plausibility of the confronting positions, and on the theoretical cogency of their defense and criticism respectively. *Namely this intention has led me to choose the suggested name of the book.*

I presume that the reader is more or less acquainted with the ideas forming the theoretical base of classical and non-classical physics, and also with the conceptual base of the main philosophical approaches to understanding the nature of space, time, and spacetime. No other knowledge of specific theoretical details or of formal language is needed for grasping the content of the book, and for assessing the strength and the plausibility of the arguments in support of the defended claims.

In the next chapter arguments are presented for the untenability of the common view of physical space and time and so for the validity of claim

(C_1) Three-dimensional space and one-dimensional time do not exist as separate autonomous entities.

The following claims are put forward in the two sections of chapter 3:

(C_2) The neglected alternative does not raise a conceptual problem for transcendental philosophy, and

(C_3) The common concepts of space and time are phenomenological.

In chapter 4 arguments are provided in support to claim

(C_4) The BA-theory of time, suggested by Lynne R. Baker, can be elaborated to become a plausible conception of time.

A central subject of analysis in chapter 5 is expressed by arguments supporting the following claim

(C_5) The growing block theory cannot account for the experience of temporal passage.

B-theorists usually share the thesis that the experienced passage of time is mind-dependent. I myself adhere to this same thesis. What is following from it is that the alleged passage of time does not really occur in nature as a physical process. This notwithstanding, one may still argue for its existence. But is this not rather a contradiction? I dare say that the answer may be negative. In section 6.3 I adduce arguments supporting the claim

(C_6) The statement about the mind-dependence of the passage of time is not completely equivalent with the statement about its non-existence.

Philosophers who maintain that time flows literally try to combat the so called no-rate argument. From this argument it follows that time does not flow at a definite rate or speed, hence it does not really flow. But there are authors who maintain that time can flow without a definite rate. In contrast to their view I support the following claim in chapter 7:

(C_7) The view that time flows literally without a definite rate exhibits conceptual flaws. The no-rate argument cannot be rejected on its ground.

Since the Newton-Leibniz debate about the substantival or the relational nature of space and time the problem is still a bone of contention among philosophers. My aim in chapter 8 is to consider three basic arguments in support of the substantival view. To this effect I raise and defend the following claim:

(C_8) In the relationalist-substantivalist debate preference has to be given to the substantival nature of spacetime.

Chapter 9 is dedicated to the curious problem about possibilities of travelling in time. Alleged ontological and logical constraints are discussed in this connection, and the following rather unexpected claim is put forward:

(C_9) Human conscious presence in the world is the genuine-and-natural time travel.

This claim stays in harmony with the elaborated BA-theory of time (see (C_4)), which stays in support of its veracity.

References in the text are given in brackets containing name of the author(s) (if not directly pointed to in the neighboring context), year of edition, and page(s); for example: (Arntzenius 2012: 125). Exceptions are the references to Kant's *Critique of Pure Reason* in the third chapter, which also include the abbreviation CPR, and the standard A and B indications for the first and the second editions, for example (Kant 1998: 27, CPR, A: 26, B: 42) where (Kant 1998) refers to Paul Guyer's and Allen W. Wood's translation of Kant's first *Critique*.

2 DO SPACE AND TIME EXIST?

2.1 The Common View of Space and Time

As Frank Arntzenius asks *prima facie* frivolously in his otherwise very serious book about space and time (2012: 125):

> We can see neither space nor time, we cannot smell them, we cannot touch them, we cannot hear them, and we cannot taste them. What, then, are these mysterious entities? Why think they exist?

People who are not physicists and/or philosophers (and even some of the latter) would probably be astonished by the very posing of this question. We can certainly not see, smell, touch, hear, or taste neither space, nor time, but nevertheless we must not be suspicious about their existence, since space and time are *somehow* directly presented to us. We see that material objects are *in space*, and we see also how they are affected by different changes occurring *in time*. So, there is no sound reason to reject the existence of space and time, and thus Arntzenius' question might be taken as some intended insidious joke.

Of course, this unproblematized view, endorsed by the "man on the street", does not mean that we can *directly* see space and time as such. This is why I used the cautious and indefinite expression that "space and time are *somehow* directly presented to us". But "the man on the street" could still be certain about the existence of space inferring it from the fact of the static positions and the dynamic behavior of things *as if* obviously being in space. At that he might have a mental representation of an (a volume of) empty space (probably a bad news for the relationalists, though they can bravely refer it to the class of the fanciful imaginations). He could also be certain about the existence of time directly inferring it from the very fact of observable changes of a *motionless* object (for instance changing its colour or temperature), and so to attribute them as occurring in time (not in space).

I shall call this view "the common-sense view of space and time", or *"the common view of space and time"* to use a shorter expression. Its basic pretention is that space and time both exist, as well as that they exist in separation from each other. The material world is grasped to be situated in a three-dimensional physical space, and to be evolving through time.

The common view of space and time has a *phenomenological background*. That is to say, one can accept by observation that perceivable phenomena are situated in space, and are changing in time. And to this effect one can further accept that space and time also exist, otherwise no phenomenon could be distinctively given to us by being observed as it is: as a concrete one, different from other phenomena (within space), and preceded and followed by other phenomena (within time). In addition, space is simply out there to encompass the configuration of all existing things at a time, while time is something separate from space and is perceived as passing (flowing).

But the common view can also be elaborated to become a conceptual base for a theoretical system. Historically, such a well-organized theoretical system is clearly discerned in Newton's classical mechanics. In its conceptual framework space and time are postulated to be absolute entities, each with its own way of existence, being independent from the material objects and their interactions. Classical mechanics is a well corroborated theory about the way objects are moving within three-dimensional space, and about the mathematical description of the forces governing their dynamic behavior. It has perfect technical applications in the world we live in, often dubbed in the literature "macro-world". And if classical mechanics is a good theory for the surrounding world, why one can bear a suspicion about the real existence of space and time? And to strengthen the question:

Why the common view of space and time is not correct?

My aim in this chapter is to present an answer to this question. I shall support the claim (C_1) denying the separate (and even more the absolute) existence of three-dimensional physical space and one-dimensional physical time.

(C_1) Three-dimensional space and one-dimensional time do not exist as separate autonomous entities.

In other words, the common view of space and time, ideologically incorporated in classical science, is a misleading conception, in spite of its usefulness in the sphere of a restricted human practice.

The arguments for this claim that will be developed below are from two different theoretical frames: from a physical point of view, and from a logical and ontological point of view.

2.2   From a Physical Point of View

As it was already said, classical mechanics is a well corroborated scientific theory about the way of motion of material objects (from tiny particles to cosmic bodies like huge stars and planets) in space and in the course of time. I'll leave aside that this theory cannot explain in detail the character of planetary orbits near a stable star, as for instance the one of Mercury, the first planet in the Sun's system. But the theory is a very successful one for explaining and predicting the kinematics and dynamics of material objects both in the world that directly surrounds us, and in the surrounding cosmic area. And this is the reason for the belief cherished during nearly three centuries by scientists and philosophers in the real existence of space and time as special autonomous entities (independent of material structures, as well as from each other). In other words, the common view of space and time was thus formed and was supported even till several decades after the birth of Einstein's special and general theory of relativity at the beginning of the twentieth century.

This was, if I can say so, the methodological reason for the acceptance of the common view of space and time. Another reason for this, as it seems, is of a cognitive character referring to the nature of human sensuous intuition. It has the ability to provide clear representation of a one-dimensional geometrical space, i.e. a line, to be ontologically related with time, and of a three-dimensional Euclidean space to be ontologically related with physical space.

A space with more than three dimensions is hardly imaginable.[1]
So, what is directly given to our eyes, or more precisely stated,
what is visualized by the mind, was traditionally accepted to be
corresponding to the real state of affairs.

However, the way contemporary scientific knowledge is growing destroys the "natural" human expectation that if we have a
clear picture of a fragment of reality as it is drawn by us through
our perceptual faculty, then it provides an adequate knowledge of
it. Contemporary scientific knowledge has however shown that we
often discern an unexpected constitution of the same fragment of
reality.

> If there was any doubt at the turn of the twentieth
> century, by the turn of the twenty-first, it was a fore-
> gone conclusion: *when it comes to revealing the true na-*
> *ture of reality, common experience is deceptive...* What
> we've found has already required sweeping changes to
> our picture of the cosmos. Through physical insight
> and mathematical rigor, guided and confirmed by ex-
> perimentation and observation, we've established that
> space, time, matter, and energy engage a behavioral
> repertoire unlike anything any of us have ever directly
> witnessed. (Greene 2011: 5, my italics)

Common experience has been deceptive for centuries for people
who were well aware that the Sun was moving around the Earth,
which was accepted to be at the center of the universe. I dare
say that the rejection of the traditional knowledge of space and
time as separately existing entities was the first step supporting the
pretension of the adduced quotation. Contemporary cosmological
descriptions of the birth and the evolution of the universe do not
rely on the common concepts of space and time, but on a theoretical
concept known as four-dimensional spacetime. Thus *the common
view of space and time was abandoned.* And nowadays cosmologists
work with ideas and theories about the history and the form of the
universe, about the so called dark energy, and seriously about the
existence of a multiverse, which go quite astray of our traditional
and classical understanding of the world.

---

[1] As Stephen Hawking (1988: 25) puts it: "It is impossible to imagine a
four-dimensional space. I personally find it hard enough to visualize three-
dimensional space!"

When I say here that "the common view of space and time was abandoned" I come to a crucial interpretative reef. It is the conviction, shared by some physicists even after the theory of special relativity was accepted, that the introduction of a four-dimensional spacetime is *merely a convenient mathematical tool* for representing the new phenomena – for example the relativity of length and time intervals for observers in different reference frames, the so called twin paradox, etc. If this conviction were taken to be true, then the instrumental feasibility of spacetime could not provide a decisive argument for claim (C_1); and one might not speak of a conclusive abandoning of the common view of space and time.

However, as it can be consistently argued, the introduction of spacetime is far more serious theoretical step than a mere adjustment of mathematical calculations. It has a clear ontological meaning. I shall briefly point to two arguments supporting this view. The one of them is the consistent construal of the fact that the relative time for observers situated in differently moving inertial systems implies also relative spaces for them.

> But when it is taken explicitly into account that relative time implies relative space, i.e. that many times imply many spaces, a basic geometrical imagination immediately demonstrates (...) that many spaces (and many times) imply a four-dimensional space with time as one of the dimensions... no relative spaces and no relative times would be possible, if spacetime did not exist. It is this basic geometric fact which demonstrates that *no relative quantities are possible without an underlying absolute reality.* In other words, the very existence of relative quantities reveals the existence of an underlying absolute reality, because the relative quantities are manifestations of that absolute reality. (Petkov 2013: 72-73, his italics)[2]

The other argument in support of the reality of four-dimensional spacetime is similar, but even more convincing. It is a corollary

---

[2] I chose to quote from this book by Vesselin Petkov (2013), because the chief aim of the author is to disclose "how the scientific picture of what exists often differs disturbingly from the "common sense" view based on the way our senses reflect the world" (see the back cover of the book), and as it is clearly seen, I also share this thesis here.

from the relativity of simultaneity. Imagine that somebody is sitting at a table, and unwillingly misplaces a glass of water very near its edge, so that the glass overturns and starts falling to the ground. The inattentive person does not certainly know if the glass will be broken or not when it reaches the floor, since this event stays in her near future. But for another observer being in motion with respect to our sitting hero, it could be the case that an unbroken glass lying on the floor near the table is an event that belongs to her present state of affairs. Well, but none of the two observers is in a privileged situation relatively to the other one. So, the fact of their own three-dimensional spaces (the one of the first observer watching a falling glass, and the other of the second observer seeing an unbroken glass on the floor), being equally existent, could be explained only by the assumption that they are three-dimensional slices from a real four-dimensional spacetime.

An additional argument for the actual existence of spacetime is adduced in section 9.4 in relation to the so called twin paradox. I placed this argument for a later discussion in another context – that of the possibility for time travels.

So, if one accepts that four-dimensional spacetime is a really existing entity, then one has to accept also the validity of (C_1). As it is known the starting date of this radical change of the scientific view of the world is the day of the historical lecture delivered by Hermann Minkowski at the 80th Meeting of Natural Scientists in Cologne on September 21, 1908, when his well-known words were pronounced:

> From now onwards space by itself and time by itself will recede completely to become mere shadows and only a type of union of the two will still stand independently on its own. (Minkowski 2012: 109)

As it seems, these words form through their figurative meaning a clever statement concerning the ontological status of space and time. It is contended that space by itself and time by itself do not exist, because they "recede completely to become mere shadows". But if something is a shadow of something else, then surely the latter is supposed to exist. No doubt, the existing entity is spacetime, while space and time by themselves, as we perceive them in experience, are mere shadows of this existing entity, although a human being is unable to perceive it in its real integrity.

However, if one follows the manner in which scientific knowledge grows, she could hypothetically presume that someday science could suspect the real existence of spacetime as well. Curious as it may seem to scholars and physicists not working in the field of quantum gravity (not to speak of laymen), this day has already come.

> String theory, loop quantum gravity, causal-set theory, twistor theory: the approaches are diverse and the disagreements among their proponents are often vehement. And yet they have a common feature: that classical spacetime is not a fundamental ingredient of the world, but a construction consisting of more fundamental degrees of freedom. Those degrees of freedom become structured in very specific ways to give rise to the observed features of classical spacetime. *This is a radical shift in our conception of physics* and its implications have yet to be fully assimilated. (Musser 2017: 217, my italics)

I shall make here some comments about the alleged "radical shift in our conception of physics".

A traditional, though not a convincing way to throw some doubt on this "radical shift" is to point to the fact that none of the enumerated theories in the adduced quotation is accepted by the scientific community to be *the* theory of quantum gravity. Yet I notice that this is not a convincing way, because some full-fledged theory could be invented in this field of research in the future, which could be probably based on the one of the mentioned theoretical approaches.

A stronger attempt at defending the fundamental status of spacetime is another meaning to be given to the ontological understanding that the so called degrees of freedom "give rise to the observed features of classical spacetime", and to go just the other way round: to assume that *they are fundamental structures of spacetime itself.* The proponents of quantum gravity theories admit these degrees of freedom to be "primitive grains of matter that do not exist within space, but simply exist" and when they string together they form space (Musser 2017: 218-219). Or they suppose "that the universe is a cat's cradle of interconnections among grains of primitive matter. Under the right conditions, extraneous connections rupture and the grains snap into a regular spatial grid" (Ibid: 221).

Two conceptual problems emerge concerning the hypothesis about the primitive grains of matter. The first one concerns the way how a material entity could exist out of space. One can imagine maybe an empty space, space without matter, but just the opposite case, material entity without any extension seems hardly imaginable. The second problem concerns the *unclear possibility for non-spatial material grains to produce spacetime*. And they are obliged to do so, since they certainly possess energy of their own to be "transformed" into the dark energy that is intrinsic for spacetime. In other words, out of the two theses that non-spatiotemporal grains and loops engender spacetime, and that spacetime is composed of some energetic structure at a deeper level, it seems, at least to me, that the second thesis is more plausible.

This way or not, what is important for the analysis here are *the arguments in support of claim (C_1)*. And succinctly formulated they are that space by itself and time by itself are simply "shadows" of spacetime (contingent elements of it associated with different observers), and thus they possess no reality of their own as separate autonomous entities. And even more, quantum gravity theorists contend that spacetime by itself is "a shadow" of something else.

2.3   From a Logical and Ontological Point of View

I shall point to an argument here in defense of claim (C_1) notwithstanding of what was already presented in 2.2. The argument comes from logic and ontology, and is expressed by the following conditional statement: if something that has been supposed to exist (for some theoretical purposes) exhibits or leads to unsurmountable paradoxes and/or logical contradictions, then this thing cannot have a real existence. So, if the common view of space and time leads our reasoning to contradictory conclusions, then we must accept that there is something wrong in this view. And inasmuch as the core assumption of the common view is that space and time exist as separate entities independently of one another, and if this assumption leads to paradoxes, then its negation would come out to be valid. And since the negation is stated by (C_1), we must admit this claim to be valid.

What remains then is paying heed to the fact that analyses of space and of time, or of space and time together, but taken as existing independently of one another, lead to paradoxical conclusions. I'll only point here to some of these analyses, since I have dwelled on them in another work of mine (Stefanov 2015: 85-120).

Maybe the most popular paradox concerning the common (dynamic) notion of time is that of John McTaggart's conclusion about the unreality of time (McTaggart 1908). But a well sustained argument for this same conclusion was suggested 19 centuries before McTaggart's attempt.

> Time is said to be tripartite – one part being past, one present, one future. Of these, the past and the future do not exist; for if past and future times exist now, each of them will be present. Nor does the present. If present time exists, it is either indivisible or divisible. It is not indivisible; for things which change are said to change in the present, and nothing changes in a partless time – e. g. iron becoming soft, and the rest. So present time is not indivisible. Nor is it divisible. It could not be divided into presents; for because of the rapid flux of things in the universe present time is said to pass with inconceivable speed into past time. Nor into past and future; for then it will be unreal, one part of it no longer existing and the other not yet existing. (Hence the present cannot be an end of the past and a beginning of the future, since then it will both exist and not exist – it will exist as present and it will not exist since its parts do not exist.) Thus it is not divisible either. But if the present is neither indivisible nor divisible, it does not exist. *And if the present and the past and the future do not exist, there is no such thing as time – for what consists of unreal parts is unreal.*[3]

And as it is also known, a similar analysis was carried out by St. Augustin as well.[4]

---

[3] Outlines of Scepticism, III, [144-146], (Empiricus 2007: 182), my italics.

[4] In his Confessions, Book eleven, XV, 20. (Augustin 1955: 184) the ancient

There are philosophers who disagree with McTaggart's conclusion about the unreality of the common notion of time (the dynamic time bearing the so-called A-properties), and others who disagree with their disagreement. But what is important for me here was already nicely expressed by Barry Dainton (2001: 18):

> However, the fact that McTaggart's argument is flawed does not mean that his conclusion is false: as we are about to see, the particular dynamic model of time he was seeking to discredit *is* deeply problematic, even if not for the reason he proposed.

The problematic character of the common notion of time is seen for instance in what B. Dainton calls the overdetermination problem. It is expressed by the absurd corollary that an event possesses and loses presentness (the tense property of an event to be a present one) at one and the same moment of time (Ibid: 20). And there are also other similar analyses disclosing the problematic character of the common notion of time (Prosser 2000).

The situation is the same concerning a strict analysis of the common notion of space. Its hidden inadequacy was revealed long ago by Sextus through an investigation of the concepts "void", "body", and "place" (Empiricus 2007: 178-179). But as it seems, the famous Zeno's paradoxes disclose in a most straightforward way the problematic character of the common view of space and time. I have shown that pretensions of different conceptual nature and theoretical potential suggested for a reasonable solution to these ancient paradoxes, but sharing a basic premise – that about the validity of the common view of space and time, are far from realizing their aim (Stefanov 2015: 87-97).

Nevertheless, because of the ontological importance of Zeno's paradoxes, I apply an *Appendix* in the end of the book, which bears the additional aim to present the most popular out of these

---

thinker writes: "If any fraction of time be conceived that cannot now be divided even into the most minute momentary point, this alone is what we may call time present. But this flies so rapidly from future to past that it cannot be extended by any delay. For if it is extended, it is then divided into past and future. But the present has no extension whatever." And so, if the present, which is said to have a real existence, has no extension, then the present would not exist, and if time is but a permanent change of present moments, then time would have no existence, too. Hence we can conclude that the dynamic concept of time is contradictory, and to this effect has no objective referent.

paradoxes, as well as to demonstrate the failure of their alleged resolutions, based on the ideology of the common view of space and time.

16

3 TRANSCENDENTAL PHILOSOPHY ABOUT SPACE AND TIME

At first glance this section may be estimated as unneeded, insofar as what is meant by space and time in the framework of transcendental philosophy is something well known for philosophers. The conceptualization of space and time is clearly presented by Immanuel Kant in his transcendental aesthetic in his first *Critique*. This being the case, my task here is not to retell known facts about the transcendental viewpoint, but to provide arguments for a claim concerning the pretension of the so called neglected alternative to demonstrate an inconsistency, or at least an incompleteness of Kant's transcendental aesthetic (see (C_2) in section 3.1), and also for a claim about the phenomenological character of the common concepts of space and time (see (C3) in section 3.2).

I assert from the beginning that claim (C_1) from the previous chapter is not valid for space and time in the context of transcendental philosophy. On the contrary, they are separate and autonomous intuitions of the knowing subject. This is so, because Kant's viewpoint inaugurates space and time not as concepts about properties or relations of things in themselves, but as pure *a priori* sensuous intuitions. Kant's clear conclusions about space in the first section of his transcendental aesthetic are:

a) Space represents no property at all of any things in themselves nor any relation of them to each other, i.e., no determination of them that attaches to objects themselves...

b) Space is nothing other than merely the form of all appearances of outer sense, i.e., the subjective condition of sensibility, under which alone outer intuition is possible for us. (Kant 1998:

159, A: 26, B: 42)

In the same way time is understood as an *a priori* intuition of
the inner sense and not as a concept for an intrinsic relation among
natural objects:

> Time is therefore merely a subjective condition of our
> (human) intuition (which is always sensible, i.e., insofar
> as we are affected by objects), and in itself, outside the
> subject, is nothing. Nonetheless it is necessarily objec-
> tive in regard to all appearances, thus also in regard to
> all things that can come before us in experience. (Kant
> 1998: 164, CPR, A: 35, B: 51)

Thus the very nature of space and time is taken to be mind-
dependent and different from the *concepts* of space and time in
physics and cosmology.

3.1 The neglected alternative

Does transcendental philosophy raise a principal barrier in front of
concepts of space and time? If such concepts could peep through
the transcendental setting, then an elucidation of the pretension of
claim (C_1) regarding them should not be relinquished.

Well, but how transcendental philosophy could allow concepts
of space and time? The possibility for this step is suggested by the
so called *neglected alternative*. It raises an objection to Kant that
even if he was right to support the transcendental ideality of space
and time, it is not excluded on principal grounds that space and
time could not pertain to things in themselves as well.

> This objection was explicitly raised by Trendelenburg
> in the nineteenth century, and it formed the basis of an
> extended and acrimonious debate with Kuno Fischer,
> the details of which have been recorded by Vaihinger.
> [...] Trendelenburg's main point was that Kant's ar-
> gument does not rule out the possibility of space being
> subjective and objective at the same time. As he ex-
> pressed the matter: "Even if we concede the argument
> that space and time are demonstrated to be subjective
> conditions which, in us, precede perceptions and ex-
> perience, there is still no word of proof to show that

they cannot at the same time be objective forms." [...
] Trendelenburg's objection is thus that, even if, for the
sake of argument, one accepts Kant's claims concerning
the apriority and subjectivity of our representation of
space, it is still perfectly possible that space itself or
spatial relations pertain to things in themselves. (Allison 1976: 313)[5]

As I already mentioned in the *Introduction*, I'll not be concerned with historical facts about the birth and development of a conception, but with its theoretical adequacy. Let me then turn to the basic idea of the neglected alternative. So, I must look for an answer to the question:

(Q_1) How things as they are in themselves could be spatiotemporal?

But as it seems to me, an appropriate step beforehand requires the posing of another question:

(Q_2) Is there anything not well systematized in Kant's transcendental aesthetic, which has provoked the idea about the neglected alternative?

For some philosophers the answer to question (Q_2) is positive, though, as we shall see, it is formal and unconvincing. This answer is based on the observation that (as we have already seen from conclusions a) and b) about the nature of space adduced at the beginning of the chapter) Kant states at first that space represents neither any property, nor any relation at all of things in themselves, and secondly, that "space is nothing other than merely the form of all appearances of outer sense, i.e., the subjective condition of sensibility". We can notice the same setting concerning the first two conclusions about time in the second section. The first conclusion a) states that "time is not something that would subsist for itself or attach to things as an objective determination, and thus remain if one abstracted from all subjective conditions of the intuition of them", and the second conclusion b) – that "time is nothing other than the form of inner sense, i.e., of the intuition of our self and our inner state..." (Kant 1998: 163, CPR, A: 32-33, B: 49).[6]

---

[5]The same order of thought can be addressed to the "perfect possibility" that temporal relations also pertain to things in themselves.

[6]Especially for time Kant presents also a third conclusion: "c) Time is the *a priori* formal condition of all appearances in general." (Kant 1998: 163, CPR,

This order of the conclusions about space and time was used for raising the opinion that Kant has derived the subjectivity of space and time from the non-spatiotemporality of things in themselves. In other words, he firstly postulates that things in themselves are not spatiotemporal, and then asserts the subjectivity of space and time in their quality of being forms of human sensibility. But as it seems the logic of the transcendental exposition ought to be the other way round. Or, in other words, Kant starts with the non-spatiotemporality of things in themselves as an unproven premise, and then concludes about the subjectivity of space and time being forms of the appearance of things in themselves that create the perceptive ability of our outer and inner sense.

This is the answer to question (Q_2) that I was seeking. Certainly, if Kant has put the cart before the horse, this disturbs the system of his transcendental aesthetic. And this formal observation comes out to be in support to the neglected alternative. I call this observation "formal" in so far as it could hardly throw any doubt on Kant's pretension that the very definition of things in themselves is based on constructing the concept of them aside from the specific way they are given to us through the *a priori* forms of sensibility – space and time.

> Paul Guyer correctly points out that the first sentence of the first conclusion denies that things-in-themselves are spatial before Kant goes on to refer to the subjectivity of space. However, whilst this is the order in which Kant's sentences go it is less clear that the order of his logical derivation is the same as the order of his sentences. The subsequent passage explicates the notion of things-in-themselves and does so only on the basis of the subjectivity of space understanding by this the fact that space has been established to be an intuition. So it appears to me that the logic of the passage is to the effect that space (and time) cannot belong to "things-in-themselves" as what is meant by "things-in-themselves" is something intrinsically non-subjective. (Banham 2009: 3)

I can add to Banham's words the clear argument made by

A: 34, B: 50)

Kant himself that it is exactly the spatiotemporality of phenomena, which makes them knowable through the forms of their givenness to our cognitive ability, i.e. through space and time. So, the non-spatiotemporality of things in themselves follows from the fact that the pure *a priori* intuitions are conditions for the human way for their representation, but in no way conditions for the possibility of the things as they are in themselves:

> Since we cannot make the special conditions of sensibility into conditions of the possibility of things, but only of their appearances, we can well say that space comprehends all things that may appear to us externally, but not all things in themselves, whether they be intuited or not, or by whatever subject they may be intuited. (Kant 1998: 160, CPR, A: 27, B: 43)

The transcendental concept of appearances in space, on the contrary, is a critical reminder that absolutely nothing that is intuited in space is a thing in itself, and that space is not a form that is proper to anything in itself, but rather that objects in themselves are not known to us at all, and that what we call outer objects are nothing other than mere representations of our sensibility, whose form is space, but whose true correlate, i.e., the thing in itself, is not and cannot be cognized through them, but is also never asked after in experience. (Kant 1998: 161-162, CPR, A: 30, B: 45)

It should become clear from this position of Kant's (and especially from his statement that "absolutely nothing that is intuited in space is a thing in itself, and that space is not a form that is proper to anything in itself") that the non-spatiotemporality of things in themselves is not an imposed prerequisite in his transcendental aesthetic, but a corollary of its basic principle that only the perceived objects in the way they are intuited by humans are in space and in time, and not things in themselves. Hence, the question (Q_2) must receive a negative answer and the following claim can be put forward:

(C_2) The neglected alternative does not raise a conceptual problem for transcendental philosophy.

The defense of (C_2) was realized up to now by the argument about the negative answer to (Q_2). I'll go on further with this defense by looking at the answer to (Q_1), asking in what sense things as they are in themselves could be grasped to be spatiotemporal.

A *prima facie* meaningful argument supporting the neglected alternative is the following: if Kant declares that things in themselves are beyond our knowledge, he could not know principally that they are not spatial and not temporal. Juan Bonaccini developed this thesis at the 20th World Congress of Philosophy along this argument.

> In fact, Kant defends the Unknowability Thesis after proving the Non-spatiotemporality one. (...) But this circumstance *is not enough* to prove that things in themselves would be necessarily non-spatiotemporal. And moreover, if it is sound, then we ought to acknowledge that Kant cannot demonstrate the Unknowability Thesis either. (Bonaccini 1998)

However, one can equally address Bonaccini with the same reasoning, but as a counter-argument. If the Unknowability Thesis is at hand in transcendental philosophy, how Bonaccini could be certain that things in themselves *are* spatiotemporal (even not necessarily, but contingently)? He could never know this, of course, since the way of existence of things in themselves stays beyond the cognitive faculties of a finite knowing subject, human, or not human. So, the only possibility that remains for Bonaccini to defend his thesis is the contention that "Kant cannot demonstrate the Unknowability Thesis either" Let me leave aside the doubt that this contention is hardly arguable. What counts for me here is the fact that the extraction of the Unknowability Thesis out from Kant's philosophy would certainly mar its transcendental setting, and hence the neglected alternative would lose any meaning.

Yet one can turn again to (Q$_1$) and raise *the hypothesis* that things in themselves can be somehow situated in space and time of their own. As it seems, this hypothesis – that comes to be in direct support to the neglected alternative – may be meaningful in two different aspects. The first one offers a *sheer speculation*, if one remains in the epistemological framework of transcendental philosophy. Knowledge about things as they are in themselves is out of the range of human cognitive capacity, but still our fantasy can admit something about them, and at that, something fundamental for their way of being as such: they are in space and time just like the objects perceived by us thanks to the pure forms of our sensibility. Such a speculation, however, is of no theoretical (not to speak of practical) value, since it can tell us absolutely nothing about what this "transcendent" space and time are. And also one can say nothing whether these imaginative space and time could be in unity, or not, concerning a claim resembling (C_1).

The second aspect in which this hypothesis could be meaningful is its strengthening with the supposition that we could come somehow to know what space and time look like even for things in themselves. But admitting the validity of this supposition is nothing less than an illegal step out of the conceptual framework of transcendental philosophy; a step toward another sort of theory of knowledge (probably a reflective one), in which the neglected alternative would simply lose its initial sense.

My aim was to defend claim (C_2), which states that the neglected alternative does not raise a conceptual problem for transcendental philosophy. And I believe that I managed to do so through the analyses of the answers to questions (Q_1) and (Q_2).

3.2 The phenomenological character of the common concepts of space and time

In section 2.1 of the previous chapter I pointed to the phenomenological background of the common view of space and time. And if, according to (C_1), the common concepts of space and time do not refer to separate physical entities, *are they specific phenomenological notions?*

From one hand, the answer may be negative, because they were transformed into working *theoretical concepts*, and not into some kind of intuitions of empirical objects, like space and time in the framework of transcendental aesthetic. From another hand, however, three-dimensional absolute space and one-dimensional absolute time have turned out to be inadequate theoretical concepts for contemporary physics, or to be "mere shadows" of the four-dimensional *spacetime*, to remember Minkowski's way of expressing their ontological unity under this accepted name (see section 2.2). Having also in mind that time, being one of the dimensions of spacetime does not really flow, notwithstanding our sense experience that time is permanently passing away, then we have enough reason to qualify the common notions of space and time as phenomenological, in so far as they are the human way to perceive a dynamical world. I'll try here to show the validity of the following claim

(C_3) The common concepts of space and time are phenomenological.

More specifically, I'll be interested in the way in which these common concepts are actually formed, if we start from the validity of transcendental philosophy, where space and time are pure *a priori* intuitions, and not concepts concerning the existence of objects *per se*. Notwithstanding this state of affairs, I'll try to suggest how space and time can acquire the use of intuitive concepts, and thus to be turned to phenomenological notions.

Strangely enough, but Kant himself uses the phrase "concepts of space and time" in connection to sensibility. When presenting the principles of a transcendental deduction in general, he writes:

> Now we already have two sorts of concepts of an entirely different kind, which yet agree with each other in that they both relate to objects completely *a priori*, namely *the concepts of space and time*, as forms of sensibility, and the categories, as concepts of the understanding. (Kant 1998: 220, CPR, A: 85, B: 118, my italics)

The first step for defending the claim that space and time could be looked upon as phenomenological concepts is to bring out their necessary role for the constitution of all objects of experience. The argument for this step has been provided by Kant himself, and it is worth noticing that he feels again the linguistic predilection to attach the word "concept" to space and time:

> Even space and time, as pure as these concepts are from everything empirical and as certain as it is that they are represented in the mind completely *a priori*, would still be without objective validity and without sense and significance if their necessary use on the objects of experience were not shown; indeed, their representation is a mere schema, which is always related to the reproductive imagination that calls forth the objects of experience, without which they would have no significance; and thus it is with all concepts without distinction. (Kant 1998: 282, CPR, A: 156, B: 195)

So, though space and time have an *a priori* representational status of a "mere schema", they are constitutive for all objects of experience. Space and time "would still be without objective validity and without sense and significance", if they (through the reproductive imagination) did not "call forth the objects of experience". Every object appears as having a specific shape of its own; two or more objects are spatially related, they are perceived or imagined to coexist in some common part of space, and within some common time interval. The transcendental ideality of space and time provides the very possibility of every empirical intuition, and to this effect, space and time are empirically real.

The second step in defense of claim (C_3) is the answer to the question "How this right-minded ontologization, no matter how much illegitimate it is from the standpoint of transcendental aesthetic, is possible?"

The only feasible answer, is that pure forms of sensibility, which make experience possible, and thus are formative for experience in "calling forth the objects", can be extracted back from experience as concepts of specific things. In a brief remark concerning the use of the notions of cause and effect in the section about the second analogy of experience within his first *Critique*, Kant admits the way of formation of concepts by emergence out of experience, pointing once again to the concepts of space and time:

> But the case is the same here as with other pure a priori representations (e.g., space and time) that we can extract as clear concepts from experience only because we have put them into experience, and experience is hence first brought about through them. (Kant 1998: 308-309, CPR, A: 196, B: 241).

Thus the mechanism of emergence of the phenomenological concepts of space and time is but their extraction "as clear concepts from experience only because we have put them into experience". As cognizing subjects we have already introduced spatial and temporal qualities within the representations of objects, i.e. we have provided the specific local space and local time order for the objects of each real or possible experience. And if this is true for *every experience*, then the formation of phenomenological concepts of space and time becomes possible. And in so far as these are the common concepts of space and time lying at the base of the common view of space and time (see the beginning of chapter 2) the argumentation for claim (C_3) has been provided.

4 A-Theory and B-Theory of Time: Is There Middle Way?

4.1 The Controversy among Theorists of Time

There are two general views on the nature of time nowadays, known as A-theory of time, and as B-theory of time, respectively.[7] These theories were named after the two time-series introduced in the well-known paper of McTaggart (1908), which challenged the reality of time.

> Positions in time, as time appears to us *prima facie*, are distinguished in two ways. Each position is Earlier than some, and Later than some, of the other positions. And each position is either Past, Present, or Future. The distinctions of the former class are permanent, while those of the latter are not. If M is ever earlier than N, it is always earlier. But an event, which is now present, was future and will be past. (McTaggard 1908: 457)

And also:

> For the sake of brevity I shall speak of the series of positions running from the far past through the near past to the present, and then from the present to the

---

[7] There are also adherents to the so called "growing block theory" pretending to account for the dynamics of the world in spacetime. To this effect it is a theory about the nature of time as well, and it will be a subject of analysis in the following chapter.

> near future and the far future, as the A series. The
> series of positions which runs from earlier to later I
> shall call the B series. (Ibid: 458)

The A-theory operates with concepts representing the usual transient temporal qualities. These are the "tensed" concepts of pastness, presentness, and futurity. The A-theorists take the flow of time, based on the permanently changing moment "now", to be (or at least to be connected to) some objective and immutable feature of time. Contrary to this assumption, B-theorists declare the flow of time to be of a subjective nature (often qualified to be mind-dependent), and to this effect they construe the experienced passage of time to be a specific illusion, accompanying the human conscious life.[8]

Different versions of both the A- and the B-theory of time have been lately suggested, but what I have here in mind is *the chief difference between them*. That is why I'll use hereafter the expression "A-theory of time" as an indication of the core claim of all dynamic conceptions of time taking the time flux to have an objective backing expressed by the usual tensed concepts (for an event to be future, present, and past). And respectively, I'll refer to the expression "B-theory of time" as presenting the core claim of all static conceptions of time – mainly that all events have their fixed positions in time, described by the relations "earlier than", "later than", and "simultaneous with". Events are actually existent in time, but they do not possess "tensed" properties as describing them to be future, present, and past events.

The A-theory offers *a dynamic view on time*, in so far as it is based on the permanently changing moment "now". Only the present events have real existence, while past events no more exist, and future events do not exist yet. The A-theory goes hand in hand with the common view of space and time. The B-theory supplies us with *a static view on time*, in so far as the temporal relations among events depicted as "earlier than", "later than", and "simultaneous with", are constant relations. On this reason the A- and the B-theory of time are known also under the headings "presentism" and "eternalism" (Baker 2010: 27), though roughly ascribed to them.

---

[8] See in this connection for instance (Paul 2012), (Prosser 2013), and (Hoerl 2014).

The controversy between the A- and B-theorists of time has still not come to an end.

The A-theory of time meets difficulties *vis-à-vis* Einstein's special theory of relativity, as well as some well-known paradoxes of the flowing time.[9] On the other hand, although the B-theory of time does not meet similar difficulties, it (still) lacks a relevant explanation why time, as being given in human experience, exhibits tensed properties, while it does not really pass as presented by an A-series.

There is a specific way out of the controversy. It is the thesis that the A- and B-theories of time (presentism and eternalism respectively) refer to different subjects that are both conceptualized as time, but in fact are ontologically different from each other, and to this effect it must be avowed that the two theories operate with two different concepts of time. Such a theoretical stance that doubles the concept of time may certainly eliminate the controversy, while supplying no satisfactory solution to it (notwithstanding the argumentative clarity of the reason for the concept multiplication).

There are also philosophers who are neither A-, nor B-theorists. I would say that they commonly fall into two categories. The first one is of "negatively minded" thinkers, who subscribe neither to the A-, nor to the B-theory of time, but who do not offer any decision alleviating, or precluding the controversy. Peter Kroes is such a philosopher who ends a paper with the following declaration: "we may conclude that the choice between minddependent and the objective theories of time flow can best be characterized as a choice between Scylla and Charybdis. Both alternatives are equally unattractive." (Kroes 1984: 445)

On the other hand, "positively minded" philosophers are seeking a middle way by suggesting a conceptual unity of the A- and the B-theory of time. Such rare attempts seem to be promising for overcoming the controversy, rather than relinquishing both "equally unattractive" alternatives in the manner P. Kroes advises us. I am in sympathy with the positively minded philosophers, like Lynne R. Baker is. So, my aim further is to reconstruct her view, and by elaborating it, to put it on more reliable grounds. Thus the chief

---

[9]McTaggart's paradox is only one of them. An inconsistency in the A-theory, due to this paradox, was also explicated by Nicholas J. J. Smith (2011). About these paradoxes see section 2.3.

aim of this chapter is putting forth and defending the following claim:

(C4) The BA-theory of time, suggested by Lynne R. Baker, can be elaborated to become a plausible conception of time.

4.2   Baker's View

According to L. R. Baker (2010: 27):

> The ontology of time is currently dominated by two theories: Presentism, according to which "only currently existing objects are real" (...), and Eternalism, according to which "past and future objects and times are just as real as currently existing ones" (...). In my opinion, neither Presentism nor Eternalism yields a satisfactory ontology of time. Presentism seems both implausible on its face and in conflict with the Special Theory of Relativity, and Eternalism gives us no handle on time as universally experienced in terms of an ongoing now.

This position clearly shows that neither the A-theory, nor the B-theory gain L. R. Baker's sympathy as full-fledged conceptions of time. But she also insists that both of the theories capture some important feature of time, which is lacking within the ontology of the other one.

> It is tempting to think that we can dispense with either the A-series or the B-series in favor of the other. On the contrary, I am convinced that we require both the A-series and the B-series to understand all the temporal facts. Neither the A- nor the B-series can be eliminated in favor of the other. (Ibid: 29)

It comes out that in order a plausible theory of time to be suggested, the dynamic aspect of the A-series ought somehow to be engrafted into the B-series of time, which is hardly controversial as a clearly outlined facet of time.[10] Thus Baker's aim is some unity

---

[10] As Lynne R. Baker puts it (2010: 31): "My aim is to take the B-series as basic, but to jack up the A-series so that it too reveals an aspect of the nature of time."

of the B- and the A-theory of time to be achieved, which she calls
"*the BA-theory of time*" (Ibid: 31). And here the problem emerges
how such a conceptual step could be safely made.

L. R. Baker undoubtedly admits that the A-series requires the
conscious assessment of any event to be either past, or present, or
future, while the ordering of the events within the B-series does
not pose such a requirement, since it presents an objective, and
not some mind-dependent ordering. However, this fact does not
cross out the experienced flow of time, although this flow does
not possess an objective backing, as a proper intrinsic aspect of
time. Well, but how is it possible the flowing time, which is not an
intrinsic property of time *per se*, to be qualified as some feature,
or aspect of time? It seems the answer to this question could be
only one. The experienced flow could be referred to time only in
the sense of a manifestation of a specific *dispositional property of
time*. And the view that Baker suggests exploits this very same
and single opportunity:

> So, to say that the A-series requires self-consciousness
> does not exclude the A-series from being an aspect
> of time. We might say that, in the absence of self-
> conscious beings, A-series are dormant (or merely po-
> tential, or latent). It is an important feature of time
> that it has a disposition toward A-properties, which
> are manifest only in relation to self-conscious beings.
> I do not see how to make sense of the world that we
> encounter without metaphysical appeal to transience;
> and the best metaphysical theory of transience, I be-
> lieve, is that its passing depends on our self-conscious
> experience. (Baker 2010: 34)

The central claim in Baker's BA-theory of time is thus *the hypothesis that the passage of time is an effect that is due to some
disposition of time to be represented as flowing*, because of the activity of human consciousness. She is convinced that

> [w]e people contribute not only to material reality, but
> to temporal reality as well. What we contribute to tem-
> poral reality are the A-series: "nowness" is a product
> of self-consciousness, but no less part of the reality of
> time for all that. (Ibid: 33)

If this central claim is accepted, the problem with the time flux may seem to be settled. But then a new problem comes to the fore. This is the problem about the nature of the assumed dispositional property of time to be perceived as flowing in human experience.[11]

4.3 The Deficiency of Baker's BA-Theory of Time

To say merely that something possesses a dispositional property is a kind of a preliminary explanation, or to say it in a better way, it is an attempt to adumbrate the course of an explanation of how a purported disposition could produce an actual result.

A dispositional property of an object does not manifest itself unless it is activated through some interaction with another object or by the characteristics of an environment. A dispositional property of a glass for instance is its fragility. If it falls, say from two meters, on hard ground, it would be broken. A safety-match has the dispositional property of being flammable. These examples of dispositional properties would not astonish the man on the street, as far as he understands the term "dispositional property" to mean a property of an object that *may appear* only when some conditions are satisfied. But the man on the street might not know *why* and *how* a dispositional property is being manifested. Such knowledge requires an explanation of the (causal) mechanism bringing about the dispositional effect. One must know e. g. the structure and properties of the chemical compound on the flammable end of the safety-match, as well as the nature of the exothermic chemical reaction, in order to explain the appearance of flame due to a strike, or heat occurring near this end.

Let me now go back to Baker's BA-theory of time. She tries to convince us that

> We cannot imagine living in a world without the passage of time. We are not just contingently related to

---

[11]L. R. Baker develops further a view called "the mixed view" in order to combine the feasible aspects of both presentism and eternalism, but this step leads her astray from the just formulated problem about the nature of the assumed dispositional property of time.

time (as we are to heat) as a cause of certain experiences. We are wrapped up in time (indeed, we are
carried away by time's winged chariot). Passing time is
the medium of our lives: To live is to get older, and to
get older is for time to pass. *There is something about
time, not just about us, that makes our experience transient.* (Baker 2010: 34, my italics)

One may find, and at least I find, the just quoted excerpt to
be a plausible assumption. But what is this "something about
time" that is always on duty to provide the flow of time in human
experience and "that makes our experience transient", provided the
B-series does not represent time as passing? As we already know a
reasonable answer is the hypothesis, embraced by Baker, that "it
is an important feature of time that it has a disposition toward
A-properties, which are manifest only in relation to self-conscious
beings".

So, there is something about time that makes our experience
transient, this "something" is *not just about us*, and to this effect
it is qualified as a disposition of time itself to be experienced as
flowing. It is a dispositional property of time *in relation* to consciousness.

So far, so good. The next step along Baker's reasoning is to
elucidate the answers of the following two questions:

1. How consciousness in relation to time induces the perception
   of a flowing time within human experience?

2. What is the nature of the attributed dispositional property
   of time?

Baker remains silent for the answers of these questions, and this
is the deficiency of her BA-theory. Without these answers, however, her idea about the perception of time as flowing to be caused
by "a dispositional property of time *in relation* to consciousness"
remains only a curious (though a heuristical) hypothesis that is
in need of further elaboration. As we have seen at the beginning
of this section, resorting to dispositions provides only a start for a
plausible explanation of the way in which a purported dispositional
property could be activated to produce some observable result.

I'll make an attempt in the following section to provide answers to both questions (1) and (2), and thus to elaborate Baker's BA-theory of time.

4.4 Attempt at an Elaboration of Baker's BA-Theory of Time

Answer to Question (1)

Let me firstly focus on the answer to question (1). The claim that is in need of an elucidation here is that consciousness induces the perception of a flowing time in relation to time proper, which does not actually flow. For all we know, the non-flowing time is represented by the B-series. So, an expounding is further needed of the conundrum how consciousness "extracts" a passage of time through its relation to the time line of the B-series of fixed temporal events. This can certainly contribute to the elaboration of Baker's BA-theory of time.

Unlike the B-series, it is the A-series that requires the conscious assessment of any event to be either past, or present, or future. This conscious assessment cannot still account for the experienced passage of time, but the A-series has a specific mechanism for this at its disposal. And this is the changing moment "now", the permanent advancement of which brings about the perception of time as flowing. If the moment "now", or the present moment for any conscious observer, requires lucid awareness of all that happens in this very moment (as well as the no less lucid awareness of her self-existence),[12] and if the moment "now" is permanently changing, then all this dynamic awareness leads to an inevitable perception of change and duration to be experienced as a passage of time. Remembering past events and expecting future ones, do certainly contribute to this experience. But the key component of the experience of time as flowing is the immutable advancement of the moment "now" .

Well, but it still remains unclear what the assertion about the

---

[12] The self-consciousness of an observer may appear to be a necessary prerequisite for her experiencing time as flowing, in so far as there is evidence that animals, and perhaps also young children, live their lives entirely in the present (Hoerl 2008).

permanent change of the moment "now" does really mean. If we concede that from the standpoint of the theory of relativity the B-series for a conscious observer is entrenched into her world-line (i.e. into her actual history through the four-dimensional spacetime), a nice construal of the assertion about the permanent change of the moment "now", or the feeling of presentness, has been suggested by Hermann Weyl:

> The objective world simply *is*, it does not happen. Only to the *gaze* of my consciousness, crawling upward along the life line of my body, does a section of this world come to life as a fleeting image in space which continuously changes in time. (Weyl 1949, 116)

This famous contention of H. Weyl, its allegorical input notwithstanding, draws an explanatory picture of the work of human consciousness to grasp consecutive three-dimensional spatial slices of the four-dimensional world corresponding to consecutive positions in time along the life line (the world-line) of a conscious being. The permanent change of the moment "now" is thus represented as a series of "sections of this world", which "come to life as a fleeting image in space which continuously changes in time". As if consciousness is advancing along one's life line illuminating consecutive states of the world at every temporal position reached by it, so that a conscious person is aware of this and only this state of the world, corresponding exactly to this temporal position, while all the remaining parts of the world are not illuminated and stay out of "the *gaze* of my consciousness". Since this famous suggestion of H. Weyl, the allegorical claim about an illuminating torch light of consciousness has been tacitly, but seriously, acknowledged by some authors. Although being a B-theorist, Barry Dainton draws a similar, but more detailed explanatory picture presenting the role of "consciousness over time":

> Imagine waking up to find yourself in a strange place. You are sitting in a field of grass, next to a lamp that illuminates the surrounding area. There is complete silence. As you look around, you can see nothing whatsoever. Apart from the small patch of grass illuminated by the lamp there is darkness everywhere. Not surprisingly, you conclude that you are alone. You could not

be more wrong. A few yards to your right there is another lamp, and another person waking up to find themselves surrounded by total darkness; likewise to your left. In fact, you are in a line of people stretching for many miles in either direction, all of whom are sitting in their own small pools of light, all of whom are alarmed to find themselves alone in a strange place.

Why is it that nobody can see anyone else? The answer lies with the strange form of light emitted by the lamps, which only extends a few feet before dying away. According to the B-theorist, we find ourselves in an analogous position in time. *What stretches only a short distance is not light through space but consciousness over time: the temporal span of direct awareness is very brief. And as in the analogous spatial case, the fact that at any given time we are not aware of experiences occurring at other times does not mean that these experiences are not there.* (Dainton 2001: 29-30, my italics)

Thus far, a definite answer to question (1) has been outlined. The experience of a flowing time is formed because of the way of functioning of human consciousness, or due to the mode in which it actively makes "sections of this world to come to life" for a conscious observer (as H. Weyl has put it).[13]

My aim, however, to consistently elaborate Baker's BA-theory of time is still not achieved. And this is so, because we have still no clarity why consciousness displays just this predilection for "crawling upward along the life line of my body", and not downward, or for behaving in some other way. There must be a specific dispositional property of time, which is responsible for consciousness to crawl upward following the direction pointing to the future events along the life line of my body. So an answer to question (2) must also be given.

---

[13] Although Weyl's idea is the only logical explanation of the subjective feeling of the permanently moving moment "now" towards the future (presupposing the macro-reality of spacetime) some details appear concerning the understanding how our consciousness is crawling through the four-dimensional world-lines of our physical bodies. These details are in need of an explanation, and a nice attempt at doing this is found in (Petkov 2013: 109-117).

Answer to Question (2)

What could be the nature of the alleged dispositional property of time? I believe that an answer to question (2) cannot be given on purely speculative grounds, concerning only the relation of consciousness to time. If such a dispositional property of time does really exist, then one may expect that its presence could be discerned somehow directly, or indirectly. And since time is a constituent of the world (at least as a specific fourth dimension of it), one may expect the dispositional property that is sought to exert a detectable influence on some of the fundamental laws of nature, being activated by interactions falling under their regulation.

Curious as it may seem, but the form of the fundamental natural laws does not imply in any way the presence of a dispositional property of time, which through the manifestation of these laws, makes even a slight difference between the past and the future direction of time (in accordance with the upward direction of time preferred by the crawling consciousness). The form of the laws is preserved when the sign of the time variable is changed; natural laws do not change with respect to this operation, they are time-reverse invariant.

But there is an exception, and this is the well-known second law of thermodynamics, which is not invariant with respect to changing the sign of the time variable. This is a clear indication that the second law of thermodynamics makes a difference between the two possible directions of time to be perceived as one pointing to the future, and the other – to the past. This is so, because according to this law the value of the entropy of an isolated physical system does never decrease, but is constantly increasing until a maximum value is reached. It is true of course, that this law of phenomenological thermodynamics has a probabilistic interpretation at a lower level within the ontology of statistical mechanics. At this level the increasing value of entropy is construed as the increasing disorder within the system. Anyhow, *the increasing entropy represents a clearly manifested natural tendency.*

> As the name suggests, the second law of thermodynamics was originally regarded as a physical *law*. Without delving into the philosophical issue about what this means, let's say that to think of the second law in this way is to think of it as having some kind of "force" or

> necessity. In some sense, what the second law dictates is
> "bound" to happen. The discovery that the second law
> is probabilistic rather than exceptionless doesn't nec-
> essarily undermine this conception. It simply means
> we need a constraint weaker than outright necessity –
> some kind of real "propensity," for example. (Price
> 2004: 222)

It is just this natural tendency of growing entropy along the time
line of consecutive states of any closed (non-interacting) physical
system, or in Price's terms, it is just this *kind of real "propensity"*,
which could represent a specific dispositional property of time. At
that, there are authors who speak of a *thermodynamic arrow of
time*, and identify this arrow as the law-like behavior of entropy to
be always increasing. But if time displays an arrow, which really
affects some natural processes to make difference between the two
possible time directions, then it could be accepted, at least provisionally, that this arrow of time is just its dispositional property
which I am looking for.

Well, but still there is a conceptual gap between the thermodynamic arrow of time, on the one hand, and the experienced flow
of time from the past to the present, and from the present to the
future, on the other hand. The experienced directed passage of
time is often dubbed "psychological arrow of time". To this effect
question (2) can be reformulated to combine the following two sub-
questions: *Do the thermodynamic and the psychological arrows of
time point at one direction, and are they interconnected?*

It is Stephen Hawking who gives a positive answer to the first
sub-question insisting that the human memory is the intermediate
link between the two mentioned arrows of time, thus providing an
answer to the second sub-question as well:

> It is rather difficult to talk about human memory be-
> cause we don't know how the brain works in detail. We
> do, however, know all about how computer memories
> work. I shall therefore discuss the psychological arrow
> of time for computers. I think it is reasonable to as-
> sume that the arrow for computers is the same as that
> for humans. If it were not, one could make a killing on
> the stock exchange by having a computer that would
> remember tomorrow's prices! ... [T]he heat expelled

by the computer's cooling fan means that when a computer records an item in memory, the total amount of disorder in the universe still goes up. The direction of time in which a computer remembers the past is the same as that in which disorder increases.

Our subjective sense of the direction of time, the psychological arrow of time, is therefore determined within our brain by the thermodynamic arrow of time. Just as a computer, we must remember things in the order in which entropy increases. This makes the second law of thermodynamics almost trivial. (Hawking 1989: 155-156)

One could be tempted to say that a good answer to question (2) has been found. As S. Hawking contends, we are conscious of past, present, and future events, since we simply remember things "in the order in which entropy increases". The second law of thermodynamics certainly demands an irreversible process, and as some authors often declare, irreversible processes determine the (thermodynamic) arrow of time. This declaration meets, however, two serious objections.

The first one is that irreversible processes are nomologically contingent because they depend on specific initial and boundary conditions, which if being settled otherwise, this would alter their course. Thus for instance, the second law of thermodynamics presupposes extremely low entropy of our universe just at the beginning of its evolution. If this were not true, then this law would not be valid. This is "the puzzle of initial smoothness of the Universe" as Huw Price calls it (2004: 228), demanding an explanation of its low entropy past. Other authors, however, maintain that the very low entropy "past state" of the universe is not in need of an explanation (Callender 2004). This being so, or not, if the specific direction of the irreversible processes is dependent on their initial boundary conditions (and it could be altered by altering the latter), then one can hardly insist that these processes *determine* the arrow of time. Rather the opposite hypothesis holds true: it is the arrow of time that is responsible for the irreversible deployment of these processes.

The second objection is connected with a mathematical result known as *Poincaré recurrence theorem*. It states that a physical system will, after a sufficiently long but finite time, return to a state very close to its initial state. Then if the system is found to be in a state of low entropy in the very outset of its existence, "after a sufficiently long time" it will reach a state with the same low entropy, which the initial state of the system has possessed. But this means that for some interval of time the second law of thermodynamics would be broken, since within this interval the entropy of the system is getting low. And if so, this law could be hardly accepted *to determine* an *arrow of time*, which supposedly does not change its direction.

Putting the statistical validity of the second law of thermodynamics aside, yet we observe the presence of a well displayed "temporal bias" in the words of Huw Price (2004: 219), referred often as "temporal asymmetry", or as "arrow of time". I have assumed at the beginning of this section that if time has a dispositional property to be manifested as a passage of time in relation to human consciousness, we could expect a specific manifestation of this same disposition (though in another manner) with respect to the form of some laws of nature. As we have seen, the second law of thermodynamics may be shown to hold just because of the presence of a temporal bias or temporal asymmetry; although this law is not responsible for it, but just the other way round, the temporal bias is responsible for the realization of this law.

However, a last step is needed for me in order to uphold the claim about the identity of the disposition (or real "propensity") of time for A-properties with its bias exhibited by the course of irreversible processes like the entropy increase. For all we know, there really is a temporal bias that is being manifested by the psychological and the thermodynamic arrows of time, as well as by the so called *cosmological arrow*, pointing to the direction in which our universe is expanding. This is the same direction of time in which the disorder of the universe, or its entropy, is constantly increasing. If we know the reason why these three arrows indicate one and the same direction of time, we might probably understand why the A-properties of time are intrinsic to our conscious experience. The solution to this problem seems so hard, as to provoke the following frank confession made by Paul Davies (1995: 278):

> Elucidating the mysterious [time] flux would, more than anything else, help unravel the deepest of all scientific enigmas – the nature of the human self. Until we have

a firm understanding of the flow of time, or incontro-
vertible evidence that it is indeed an illusion, then we
will not know who we are, or what part we are playing
in the great cosmic drama.

In connection to the last words of this quotation, it is my claim
that the solution to the problem why the three arrows of time
possess one and the same direction, and to this effect why time
exhibits clear directional asymmetry, *bears a global cosmological
character.*

It is no wonder that the cosmological arrow, indicating the time
direction in which the universe is expanding, is caused by the initial conditions immediately after the Big Bang. I have in mind the
specific value of the cosmological constant, the so called inflation
period, in which our universe has undergone an enormous expansion, and other similar factors that refer to the universe as a whole.
As we already know, the thermodynamic arrow has also a cosmological pre-condition for its directedness; and this is the very low
entropy at the start of the universe.

What then about the psychological arrow due to which we remember past events, but not future ones? Does it presuppose a
cosmological reason as well?

If S. Hawking is right that "we must remember things in the
order in which entropy increases", and "this makes the second law
of thermodynamics almost trivial", then we may assume that the
cosmological pre-conditions for both the cosmological and the thermodynamic arrows are the same for the psychological arrow of
time, as well. *The disposition of time for A-properties is the same
temporal asymmetry, which determines the indication of the other
two arrows.* It is true that we know very little about how human
consciousness is functioning staying in relation to time, and the
time flux seems "mysterious" to us, to use P. Davies' qualification.
But I can point to at least two reasons for my contention that the
disposition of time for A-properties is identical with the same temporal asymmetry, which determines the indication of the other two
arrows of time (the thermodynamic and the cosmological one).

The first reason is of a formal character and is based on the
Ockham's razor principle. The presumption that an observable
time asymmetry is also a disposition of time for A-properties (or
for the experiencing of time as flowing) is to be preferred to the

presumption that time exhibits two directional asymmetries different from each other: the one responsible only for the psychological
arrow, while the second – for the other two arrows of time.

The second reason is of a substantial character, since it concerns
the very existence of human beings within the universe who do have
the experience of time as flowing. Though based on the so called
weak anthropic principle, the strong argument here is that intelli-
gent beings could not exist in a universe, in which the cosmological
and the thermodynamic arrows of time are counter directed.

> Why do we observe that the thermodynamic and cos-
> mological arrows point in the same direction? Or in
> other words, why does disorder increase in the same di-
> rection of time as that in which the universe expands?
> If one believes that the universe will expand and then
> contract again... this becomes a question of why we
> should be in the expanding phase rather than the con-
> tracting phase.

> One can answer this on the basis of the weak anthropic
> principle. Conditions in the contracting phase would
> not be suitable for the existence of intelligent beings
> who could ask the question: Why is disorder increas-
> ing in the same direction of time as that in which the
> universe is expanding? (Hawking 1989: 159-160)

So, the second reason for my claim that the disposition of time
for A-properties coincides with the temporal asymmetry, which determines the cosmological and the thermodynamic arrows, is that
if the latter two arrows do not point to one and the same direction
of time, then human beings would not exist, and thus the problem
of the "mysterious time flux" would not appear. But the cosmological characteristics of our universe are such and not others, so
that human beings to appear at some stage of its history. And this
is just the brief formulation of the weak anthropic principle.[14] Put
into the thematic context of my interest here, I may reformulate
the principle in the following way: the cosmological characteristics
of our universe are such and not others, so that the psychological

---

[14]In order to survive, living creatures (human beings included) must consume
energy in an ordered form, through feeding for instance, and to convert it into
heat, which is a disordered form of energy. Cf. (Hawking 1989: 160).

arrow of time to be an immutable part of human conscious experience. My claim that it is one and the same asymmetry of time to determine the direction of its three arrows gains a defense, and hence this fundamental temporal asymmetry is also the disposition of time for A-properties that was looked for. Thus question (2) has received a plausible answer.

In the end the following conclusion can be done:

Lynne R. Baker claims that each of the competing A- and B-theory of time, though separately unsatisfactory, captures some important aspect of time. Being convinced that "it is an important feature of time that it has a disposition toward A-properties, which are manifest only in relation to self-conscious beings", she offers a BA-theory of time to combine the properties of the A- and B-series of time. I accept the underlying idea of the BA-theory, but I also find that it displays a non-trivial conceptual deficiency. It is the lack of answers to questions (1) and (2) respectively: "How consciousness in relation to time induces the perception of a flowing time within human experience?", and "What is the nature of the attributed dispositional property of time?"

The answer to the first question is focused on giving an interpretation for the feeling of a permanently changing moment "now", which induces the perception of a flowing time. The answer to the second question was to provide relevant argumentation that the dispositional property of time that is looked for is identical with the temporal asymmetry, or temporal bias, exhibited by the thermodynamic and the cosmological arrows of time. The answers to both of the questions (1) and (2) were needed for an extended elaboration of Baker's BA-theory of time. In this way claim (C_4) was defended, which was the chief aim of this chapter.

*

Philosophical curiosity concerning the elaborated BA-theory of time might be expressed by putting forward the question:

Why there is time asymmetry?

This question does not directly affect the content of the elaborated BA-theory of time, since it was enough for me to identify the disposition of time for A-properties with the exhibited time asymmetry. It is expressed by the already presented three arrows of time. In so far as they point to one and the same direction, I can speak here about *the arrow of time*, having in mind primarily the cosmological arrow.

As it seems a possible answer to the above question could refer to some fundamental quality of our universe. This certainly shows the importance of posing the question, as well as the difficulty for reaching an arguable answer. Yet I shall try to propose one.

In so doing I direct my attention to the symmetries reining the micro-world, or the world of quantum phenomena. As it is known a system of elementary particles exhibits a CPT-symmetry. This means that it is invariant, i.e. will stay the same, when subjected to three simultaneous transformations: changing the elementary particles with their respective anti-particles (which would change their electric charges with the opposite ones), indicated by "C", a mirror transformation of the system, indicated by "P", and changing the sign of the time variable, indicated by "T". If one of these transformations is not applied, the system could prove not to stay invariant.

In the early stage of the evolution of the universe elementary particles and anti-particles were born, but later the material structures of our visible universe were made only by particles, and not by anti-particles. This means that the CP-symmetry in the early universe proves to be broken, although in a very small scale: after a vehement annihilation among one billion particles and the same number of respective anti-particles, one particle managed to remain. Yet this was enough for complex material structures to appear being constructed by protons, neutrons, and electrons. *Matter has overcome anti-matter.* Well, but in my view, this asymmetry, which has given birth to a universe with material (and not anti-material) planets, stars, galaxies and huge galactic configurations, was compensated by an additional asymmetry – that of time, so that the CPT symmetry to be valid. Thus time obtained an arrow pointing the direction of the universal expansion. If I may say so, the "price" for the material universe, for the non-empty universe (filled up entirely by pure energy), is the arrow of time, or as Paul Davies (1995: 213) has put it, that our universe is "lopsided".

This lopsidedness, as well as the breaking of the mirror symmetry in the quantum world, are not so strong, so that the universe to be almost symmetrical, and not so weak, so that the universe to be not empty of matter having a propensity to evolve.

This is my idea for the answer to the fundamental cosmological question "Why there is time asymmetry?"

5 THE GROWING BLOCK THEORY

Almost every physical theory works with a concept of time that is formally inscribed within its mathematical apparatus. The *fundamental problem* what is the real nature of time (and of spacetime), however, is left for a more abstract theoretical reasoning, and chiefly for philosophy (metaphysics).

We have already seen in section 4.1 that there are two different metaphysical conceptions about the nature of time. The first is a *dynamic one*, and is elaborated by different, so called A-theories of time. The proponents of this conception admit that in a way time is really flowing. And if this is the case, then there appears no problem about explaining the human experience of time passage. This conception stays in harmony with classical physics (classical Newtonian mechanics) and admits that the world is three dimensional and is evolving through time.

However, as it was shown in 2.1, this conception is obsolescent against the background of the ontology of the special theory of relativity. And in 2.2 it was also shown that the dynamic conception of time or the A-theory of time in general, is confronted with different kinds of paradoxes.

The second conception of time, *the static one*, is elaborated by different, so called B-theories of time. Time is usually represented as a dimension of a unified physical reality – the spacetime. This way or not, but the central point within this conception is that time ceases to be accepted as really flowing.

Probably attracted by a linguistic fashion for metaphorical brevity, some philosophers refer to these two rival conceptions by using the labels "presentism" and "eternalism" (see the beginning of 4.2).

Fortunately, the static conception stays in harmony with the ontologies of the special and of the general theory of relativity. Besides, it does not meet paradoxes, characteristic for A-theories of time, namely because they operate with concepts of tensed properties that lack objective meaning (a future event will become present, and then will become past one for a concrete observer). To this effect it could be concluded that it would be rational to say adieu to the dynamic conception and to embrace the static one (eternalism).

However, even if this conclusion is right, one might still have no good reason to maintain that in case presentism is rejected, it necessarily follows from this that we must accept automatically the validity of eternalism. It is true that it does not lead to paradoxes like those implied by the ontology of the flowing time, but it is also broadly accepted that the theory fails to explain the conundrum why time seems to pass, if it does not do so. In other words, the experience of the passage of time poses a challenge for B-theorists. Besides, eternalism represents a *block-universe*, which is somehow reluctantly accepted by some thinkers, probably because of existential considerations.

At the background of the embarrassments just mentioned, a third conception about the nature of spacetime has emerged – the so called *growing block theory*, or *growing block* for short. Though rarely, it is also dubbed *growing blockism* (Miller 2013: 348). It shares parts of the ontology of both the static and the dynamic conception of time. To this effect it is expected that this theory could provide a better understanding of the nature of time. And if so, one could also expect that the growing block is in a position to explain why time is perceived by us to be flowing.

I'll further try to show that this expectation does not hold water; and I'll thus try to argue for the following claim:

(C$_5$) The growing block theory cannot account for the experience of temporal passage.

According to the growing block theory, the physical world is but a dynamic block of four-dimensional spacetime filled up with material structures, which permanently enlarges its scope. This means that thus the world remains static regarding all its states belonging to the past, while it is intrinsically dynamic regarding all its present and future states.

[S]uch a theory as this accepts the reality of the present

and the past, but holds that the future is simply nothing at all. Nothing has happened to the present by
becoming past except that *fresh slices of existence have
been added to the total history of the world.* The past is
thus as real as the present. (Broad 1923: 66, my italics)

This is the core thesis of the growing block, made by Charlie
Broad – the initiator of this view. Later, it has been elaborated by
Michael Tooley (1997) by the use of a tenseless, though a dynamic
scheme of time. But even his elaborated view attracts different objections, including semantic issues on the truth values of sentences
with their objects referring to concrete moments of time (Mellor
1998: 81-83).

I'll not pay attention here to a semantically based criticism. My
intention is to show that the growing block (notwithstanding its
pretention) can hardly explain why we have an experience of time
as flowing. My criticism is based on theoretical considerations.

If the physical world is accepted to be a growing block, then
it is a natural assumption our experience of temporal passage to
be related to the real way of growing of the spatio-temporal block.
*Time flow is thus explained by the process of addition of new slices
of existence onto the block.* This being the case, however, one has
to elucidate how the process of addition of new slices onto the
space-time block is being realized.

As Barry Dainton has rightly noticed, the contention about the
permanently accreting "slices of existence" is liable to two possible
interpretations. The first one states that

Past, present and future moments of time are equally
real and permanent, but may be empty. As events are
created, time is gradually filled with concrete events.
(Dainton 2001: 70)

This interpretation raises an overdetermination problem. If it
were right, each moment of time could be both empty of events
(when it is not yet reached by the material growth of the block),
and not empty of events (when it is reached by the process of
material growth of the block). But since a given moment of time
could not be thought of being both deprived of material events and
also to be attributed to concrete events, this interpretation has to

be abandoned. So, the growing block theorists must subscribe to the other possible interpretation:

> Moments of time come into being with things and events; there are present and past moments, but no future moments. (Ibid)

This interpretation evades the overdetermination problem of the previous one. The accreting slices become real together with their own "corresponding" times and thus the growth of the spatio-temporal block is being realized.

The curious question then can be posed: *"How fast does the block grow?"*

> However, if times and their occupants come into being together, this question has no real sense. The question "How much time passes between the addition of one reality-slice and the next?" would be perfectly meaningful if a block-universe existed in an external time dimension (...). But since the block theorist recognizes (or should recognize) no such external time, all we can say is that successive phases of reality come into being at (and along with) the times when they occur. That a specific speed cannot be produced in response to the "How fast?" question is something taken to be disastrous (or at best a serious embarrassment) for the growing block theory. (Ibid: 71)

But let us suppose that the universal block grows at some definite rate, or better say, has its own objective dynamics of enlargement (since the notion of rate presupposes implicitly an "external time"). Then it can be contended that this rate, or directed dynamics, could be taken to provoke in some way or another subjective feeling of time passage. My claim is that this contention can hardly be taken to be true, *neither from a psychological, nor from a physical point of view.*

For one reason, the subjective human experience of time passage does not seem to be fixed. It depends on our emotional states initiated by different life conditions.

And for another reason, because of the fact that for two observers, being in relative motion to one another, an event lying into the future of the first observer can be a present event for the second one. This is a well-known corollary from the theory of special relativity, because two observers in relative motion to one another have different sets of simultaneous events. Then such an event *must not exist for the first observer*, since according to the growing block theory, future events possess no real existence; while *the same event is taken to be quite real for the second observer.*

Along the line of this reasoning the following two claims come to the fore:

(1) The concept of real existence becomes relative, and

(2) The *subjective* feeling of time passage may vary, while the dynamics of the spatio-temporal block is *objective* and thus a common one for all conscious inhabitants of the world.

Claims (1) and (2) obviously represent serious impediments in front of the standard growing block theory. They lead to the conclusion that this theory cannot explain the human feeling of time passage.

Let us take the central thesis of the growing block seriously, i.e. let us accept the way in which the world is said to be growing in scope. As a preliminary argument for this step one may point to the paradigmatic claim made by contemporary cosmologists that our universe is an expanding world.

Well, but in case one does not willingly admit the relativization of reality as a consequence from claim (1), as well as the embarrassment stated by (2), one ought to admit that the *perception of time as flowing* could be a fact even in a spatio-temporal block which is not growing, i.e. within the theoretical context of eternalism. This intrinsic perception of human consciousness must be liable then to another explanation, *different* from the assumption that the block universe is enlarging its scope step by step, or more "correctly" said, "slice by slice".

Another curious situation can also be discerned. As it is known, the expansion of our universe does not proceed with one and the same rate. Most cosmologists say that an acceleration of the universal expansion has been registered. Does this mean – if the expansion is due to a permanent piling of slices of existence – that *the experienced passage of time* will undergo a corresponding parallel change as well? An objection could here be raised that this, otherwise clear question does not presuppose a clear answer, since if our subjective feeling of time passage is provoked directly by the universal expansion, any observation of a change of our human subjective feeling would be impossible. But even if this were true, the very posing of the question is not meaningless.

Can we seek a place of refuge in the expectation that there is something not well accommodated within the theory of the growing block, which could be evaded by a convenient additional theoretical improvement? The latter should be able to cope at least with the relativization of reality following from claim (1).

A rescue strategy for the growing block theory could certainly be found. It should presuppose the attraction of some new auxiliary assumption elaborating conveniently the very notion for a dynamic slice of reality. The auxiliary assumption can take the form of an additional postulate. It should explicate a regulative constraint by stating that the accreting slices of reality have some well-defined thickness, allowing one and the same event to be both present for some observers, and future for other ones. So, situated *within* the slice that forms the present state of the world the event has an objective existence by definition. This postulate copes *prima facie* with the relativization of reality.

However, this postulate is but a genuine *ad hoc* hypothesis. The supposed thickness of the slices is a *purely arbitrary assumption*, in so far as it is not an empirical consequence from any theoretical principle typical for the ontology of the growing block theory. For instance, the well-known Andromedean illustration proposed by Roger Penrose for presenting the relativity of simultaneity would fail, because the accreting slices of reality should not be of such "unreasonable" thickness.[15]

Independently of what has been said up to now, I can point to another serious obscurity in the theory of the growing block. This is the lack of explanation of the implicitly taken (in the sense of not rejected by the growing block) proviso that the permanent piling of the slices of reality onto the already existing space-time block must

---

[15] The relativity of simultaneity is illustrated by R. Penrose in the following way: For one of two observers, walking past each other along the street, a fleet from a distant place in Andromeda has just started its flight to invade the Earth, while for the other observer the decision about the invasion has not yet been taken, and the Andromedean space ships are still not flying. Both of these events in relation to the two observers are equally real, notwithstanding the several days' time interval between them. (Penrose 1989: 260-261)

be produced in such a manner, which strictly conforms to the causal law, as well as to the manifestation of the huge amount of observed irreversible processes. The obscurity is expressed firstly by the need to *impose the causal law* on the already existing present events in relation to the yet *non-existing* future ones, which will build the structure of the *not yet materialized slice of reality*, coming next after the present slice. And secondly, the obscurity is expressed as well by the need to set out *a priori* directions of irreversible processes (which could principally have an arbitrary duration, exceeding that of the accreting slices of reality).

In the end yet another embarrassment can be revealed. I mentioned above that the contemporary cosmology of our expanding universe could be taken to stay in support to the growing block theory. However, the specific "mechanisms" through which our universe is enlarging its scope within the two theoretical models are quite different. Indeed, without going into any details, one ought to notice that the expansion of the universe is said to be due to the "anti-gravitational" nature of the so called dark energy, intrinsic to the universal spacetime. Thus every consecutive stage of the universe is connected to the previous one not by the addition of a slice of reality coming from nothingness (as is the case with growing blockism), but by a process of enhancing the distances among existing galaxies (and more generally speaking, among and within material structures). This being the case, the contemporary cosmological paradigm comes out to be of no support to growing blockism.

The arguments set out here lead me to *the conclusion* that the growing block theory cannot account for the experience of time passage. In other words, claim (C_5) has received a proper argumentation.

Let me remind in the end that *the elaborated BA-theory of time* presented in the previous chapter has the pretension to explain human experience of time passage. And in so far as it is consistent with the four-dimensionalism of the theory of relativity, it is a candidate for a plausible conception of time.

6 THE PHENOMENOLOGY OF TEMPORAL PASSAGE

6.1 Preliminary Words about the Mind-Dependence of Temporal Passage

The bone of contention among philosophers of time is *the acceptance or the rejection* of the belief that temporal passage is an objective feature of time. Concerning the answer to the question "Does time really flow?" there is a huge controversy. And the dividing line within the set of competing theories of time is not only between the strict presentist wing in the range of the A-theories that defend what has been recently called "robust passage of time", and the strict eternalist wing of the B-theorists, supporting the conception about the actuality of a block universe without flow of time whatsoever.[16] There are philosophers in between this mutually excluding positions concerning the alleged reality of temporal passage.

B-theorists usually support the thesis that the experienced passage of time is mind-dependent. I myself adhere to this same thesis. But I also stay behind the opinion that even this being so, the mind-dependence, or the phenomenological cognitive status of the passage of time, does not yet present a simple argument for a complete rejection of the existence of this phenomenon. If somebody is saying that the experienced passage of time is mind-dependent, what is at most following from this statement is that the alleged passage of time does not really occur in nature as a physical pro-

---

[16] About the A- and the B-theory of time see section 4.1.

cess. This notwithstanding, one may still argue for its existence. But is this not rather a contradiction?

I dare say that the answer may be negative. In section 6.3 I'll adduce arguments to this effect by defending the claim

(C_6) The statement about the mind-dependence of the passage of time is not completely equivalent with the statement about its non-existence.

Before this attempt, however, I shall have a look at a group of theories covered by the heading "the moving spotlight theory". I ought to do so because of the fact that these theories have the pretension to solve the problem of time flow by accepting the reality of the latter, and thus the debate about the construal of its mind-dependence loses its philosophical significance.

6.2　The Moving Spotlight Theories

The so called *moving spotlight theories* (MSTs) seem, at first glance, to settle the situation with the discussed problem about the passage of time. At a second glance, however, as I shall try to show briefly, MSTs exhibit deficiencies that hamper their intended purpose.

A moving spotlight theory (MST) conforms to Einstein's theory of relativity in accepting the thesis that future, present, and past events share equal ontological status (in so far as they are equally present in a four-dimensional spacetime). Thus such a theory seems to be a promising one, since at the same time it provides a suggestion about the way time passage can be grasped as a real process of an ever advancing present moment of time.

In the words of Kristie Miller (2018: 1):

> I take the moving spotlight theory (MST) to be the conjunction of three theses: (a) past, present and future objects, properties, and events exist and (b) a privileged proper sub-set of these objects, properties, and events instantiates presentness, and (c) which objects, properties and events instantiate presentness, changes. Further, I assume that temporal passage consists in the movement, or (as I will henceforth say), *change* of presentness.

It comes out that the main thesis characterizing each MST is the one about the movement of the feature of presentness. Why then these theories of time are not called moving presentness theories (or theories of the moving presentness), but are recognizable under the name of moving *spotlight* theories?

As it seems, the answer points to a consensual agreement among philosophers of time to raise the name "moving spotlight theory" being inspired by a convenient comparison once made by Charlie Broad for an allegorical presentation of the advancing presentness through time:

> We are naturally tempted to regard the history of the world as existing eternally in a certain order of events. Along this, and in a fixed direction, we imagine the characteristic of presentness as moving, somewhat like the spot of light from a policeman's bull's-eye traversing the fronts of the houses in a street. What is illuminated is the present, what has been illuminated is the past, and what has not yet been illuminated is the future. (Broad 1923: 59)

Well said, but appealing to our intuition by using an allegorical analogy cannot serve, regretfully, as an arguable theoretical account. This being the case, *the crucial point* in each version of MST is the theoretical development of its general statement about the permanently changing temporal property called *presentness*.

Bradford Skow gives names of three MSTs that he considers in his recent book (2015): "the moving spotlight theory with supertime", or "MST-Supertime" for short, "MST-Supertense", and MST-Time.

It is my opinion that only the first theory develops a conceptual scheme that could be accepted as ontology capturing temporal passage. It is well known what it means for one to say that something, say a ball, is flying, i.e. is moving through space. This means that the ball is occupying a volume of space relatively to each moment of its flight. But can we say the same thing about time when insisting that it also flies, or moves? Certainly the answer is negative. Firstly, because time is not supposed to move through space, and secondly, because we lack another temporal dimension to secure a linear set of indeces relative to which proper time is moving. Adherents to MST-Supertime cope with the second difficulty by introducing supertime to play the role of the missing temporal dimension. Thus they say that at each point of supertime exactly one instant of time is present (Skow 2015: 46). But the suggested ontological picture does not finish with the introduction of supertime only, since the first difficulty ought to be overcome as well. This means that an answer must be given to the question through what does time move, if it does not move through space. So, an additional temporal dimension is added into the picture notwithstanding its complication, but for the sake of an explanation how a real passage of time could be realized. The "usual" time is renamed as "B-time" and the temporal dimension through which B-time is moving is named "A-time". Thus MST-Supertime says that different points of supertime are correlated with different B-time's locations in A-time. For instance, at later points of supertime B-time has moved farther along A-time.

This is in a lapidary presentation the ontological picture of MST-Supertime explaining the real passage of time. The skepticism about its acceptance stems, as it seems, not so much from its ideological resemblance with the way physical bodies move through space with respect to time, lacking any sound knowledge whether temporal passage could be depicted in a similar way. The skepticism stems from its strong ontological commitments, resembling the status of *ad hoc* hypotheses, as the introduction of supertime, A- and B-time, as co-existing. I completely agree to this effect with Bradford Skow's (2015: 49) assessments:

> I think the theory is completely ridiculous. I just cannot bring myself to take it seriously as a theory of the world that might well be true. I am willing to believe in the existence of time, but not in the existence of both B-time and A-time... I have already complained that belief in supertime is just too much to ask.

Indeed, MST-Supertime is based on naïve assumptions, which involve "ridiculous" ontological requirements about additional temporal entities, whose contrived existence is far from really detectable in the natural world.

What about the other two MSTs, which B. Skow dubs "MST-Supertense", and "MST-Time"? The first theory does not use the idea of supertime, but relies instead on the introduction of "super tense operators", and thus uses a language that preserves a typical A-vocabulary. This language could be rendered in principle into sentences using the natural language with tensed properties (pastness, presentness, and futurity), if needed. I am not going to consider MST-Supertense here, because of two reasons. The first is trivial: the theory is presented in detail by B. Skow (2015: 50-58), so there is no need for superfluous repetitions. The second reason is important for me. And it is the fact that the theory deals mostly with semantical issues like truth values of sentences referring to events happening in time. It remains silent about constructing an ontological model of the way the property presentness permanently advances along the time dimension. This has been done by MST-Supertime, though unsuccessfully. And this is what I'm mostly interested in.

The same words go well about MST-Time, exposed by B. Skow (Ibid: 58-68). It also deals with collection of sentences stating what reality looks like from the perspective of an instant of time, and their truth-values. But the answer to the question how the "spotlight" or, that is to say, presentness is really moving is left without an ontological elucidation.

The pretension of Kristie Miller is to provide such an elucidation by revealing how the movement or the change of the feature of presentness is being realized. She offers to this effect a new MST called "the cresting wave", and starts with a confidence to our phenomenology of temporal passage. After the quoted claims at the beginning of this section she develops an argument from passage phenomenology, based on an inference to the best explanation (Miller 2018: 2):

(a) We have experiences as of the passage of time.
(b) If we have experiences as of the passage of time, then the best explanation for this relies on the passage of time being an objective feature of reality.

Therefore:

C: The passage of time is an objective feature of reality.

The key sub-argument in support of K. Miller's theory is that "in the absence of temporal passage our phenomenology would not be passage phenomenology" (Ibid.). I can say, the other way round, that *in the presence* of objective temporal passage it is almost certain that our phenomenology would be passage phenomenology.

But *in the absence* of objective temporal passage our phenomenology would either not be, or *could happen to be* passage phenomenology. I share the conviction that the last possibility is the case, but K. Miller rejects it, because it leads to the conclusion that the experienced passage of time turns to be an illusion, which is an unacceptable alternative. I'll present my comments concerning this alternative in the next section. What is here more important is that the temporal passage is understood as the permanent change of presentness, and to this effect K. Miller (2018: 9) formulates the following principle:

> **Distinguishability Principle**: Typically, for any time *t*, at *t* subjects have a phenomenology as of presentness when, and only when, *t* instantiates presentness.

Then she meticulously examines whether extant kinds of MSTs (classical and non-classical) that seem to be plausible are consistent with the Distinguishability Principle, and reaches a *negative answer*. And this is the reason for her to propose a new theory called, as I have already mentioned, *the cresting wave theory*. To tell her story K. Miller introduces firstly the concept of fundamental properties being manifested at a moment of time *t*, the property of presentness being one of them. And in so far as presentness differs in an essential way from other fundamental properties, a set of fundamental-minus properties is defined to be "the set of all of the fundamental properties of a world, except for the property of presentness" (Miller 2018: 18). On the base of this definition the cresting wave theory receives a succinct formulation:

> Let δ be the set of *t*'s fundamental-minus properties when *t* is future, and ϕ be the set of *t*'s fundamental-minus properties when *t* is present, and γ be the set of *t*'s fundamental-minus properties when *t* is past. We can then characterize the cresting wave theory as follows
>
> Cresting wave theory: (a) $\delta \neq \phi$ and (b) $\phi \neq \gamma$ and (c) $\gamma \neq \delta$. (Ibid: 20)

This formulation is consistent, but let me remind that the phenomenology of temporal passage is in effect the phenomenology as of presentness, and so the crucial element of the cresting wave theory is the explanation of the process of time's instantiation of presentness (see the Distinguishability Principle). The locution "t instantiates presentness" is quite general and to this effect uninformative. Some ontology ought to be attracted for the elucidation of how presentness is being instantiated. And here is K. Miller's metaphysical decision:

> One way, but not the only one, is to appeal to dispositions. Henceforth I will understand dispositions as powers that can be manifested. Further... I will suppose that it is properties that do the causal work, and that causation is the result of powers manifesting themselves. Causation is the result of suitable powers appropriately combining and manifesting; effects are brought about by powers working together to manifest some further property. I call the version of the cresting wave theory spelled out in terms of this framework, the *manifesting wave theory* (MWT).

The MW theorist holds that presentness is an essential component of *any* combination of powers that manifest. So what it is for a moment to be present is for its dispositional properties to manifest. What it is for a moment to be future is for its dispositional properties to be as yet unmanifested, and what it is for a moment to be past is for its dispositional properties to have been manifested: for those properties to be spent. (Ibid: 21)[17]

K. Miller's MWT appeals to *dispositions* to be understood as "powers that can be manifested". Properties are taken to be the causal agent, but "causation is the result of powers manifesting themselves". And what is essential for the instantiation of presentness at a moment is the requirement for this moment "its dispositional properties to manifest", while presentness is posited as "an essential component of *any* combination of powers that manifest".

All this could be certainly taken as some convenient metaphysical story of how presentness is being instantiated. But the story relies on a scheme providing only a general conceptual frame of how presentness comes to the fore at every moment of time in order the

---

[17] K. Miller considers mainly two versions of MWT – pandispositionalism and moderate MWT, depending on whether the MW-theorist accepts that there are some permanent fundamental properties in the four-dimensional block, or not. See for instance (Miller 2018: 23).

phenomenology of temporal passage to be explained. Probably because of this K. Miller (2018: 26) writes in the end of her, no doubt, original paper:

> Of course, one might think that the cresting wave theory is metaphysical craziness. As it happens, I agree. But if that is your view, then either you, like me, should reject the MST altogether or, if you endorse that view, you should do so for reasons other than an appeal to the content of our passage phenomenology.

This final conclusion is an avowal that MSTs cannot account for the phenomenology of temporal passage, except the cresting wave theory. However, its conceptual base is contestable. In what follows (till the end of this section) I'll try to show that this is the case, by putting forth three main arguments.

The first one is that the supposed cresting wave carrying the special quality of presentness along consecutive moments of time is at odds with the relativistic notion of presentness. It is tacitly accepted that this wave is advancing through the whole four-dimensional block. According to the special theory of relativity every observer has its own present moments along its four-dimensional world line. But this means that there should be as many cresting waves with their own mechanism of manifesting dispositions, as is the number of all observers being in relative motion with respect to each other; and this really seems to be a crazy picture.

The second argument that throws a shadow of suspicion on the cresting wave theory is very similar to the overdetermination problem stated by B. Dainton with respect to an interpretation of the growing block theory (criticized in ch. 5 as a theory pretending to account for the phenomenology of temporal passage). As we know, according to this interpretation "past, present and future moments of time are equally real and permanent, but may be empty. As events are created, time is gradually filled with concrete events" (Dainton 2001: 70). However, this interpretation raises an overdetermination problem. If it were right, each moment of time could be both empty of events (when it is not yet reached by the material growth of the block), and not empty of events (when it is reached by the process of material growth of the block). But since a given moment of time could not be thought of being both empty of material events and also to be attributed to concrete events, there appears an overdetermination problem.

In so far as every MST accepts that "past, present and future objects, properties, and events exist",[18] so does MWT. In other words, time actually exists in the block universe. But as we already know, according to MWT "what it is for a moment to be present is for its dispositional properties to manifest. What it is for a moment to be future is for its dispositional properties to be as yet unmanifested" (Miller 2018: 21). So it turns out that every moment of time is associated with both manifested and yet unmanifested dispositional properties. Thus every moment of time comes to be associated with two different physical states of the world. And this raises an overdetermination problem.

The third argument is concerned with K. Miller's suggestion about the introduction of *dispositional properties*. From one side, they play a key role in bringing about presentness at every consecutive moment of time. This is so, because they are identified with "powers that can be manifested", and presentness is posited as "an essential component of *any* combination of powers that manifest". Thus *presentness is unachievable without the manifestation of the alleged powers* that permanently are manifesting themselves from one moment of time to the following one. From another side, however, this general metaphysical picture displays a dearth of a required explanation about the nature of the attracted dispositional properties, the function of which resembles the role of *ad hoc* hypotheses in scientific knowledge.

It is a fact that I have also looked for a dispositional property when I proposed an elaborated version of the BA-theory of time. However, in section 4.3 a necessary elucidation was provided how a dispositional property could manifest itself:

"A dispositional property of an object does not manifest itself unless it is activated through some interaction with another object or by the characteristics of an environment. A dispositional property of a glass for instance is its fragility. If it falls, say from two meters, on hard ground, it would be broken. A safety-match has the dispositional property of being flammable. These examples of

---

[18]See the first quotation by K. Miller (2018: 1) at the beginning of this section.

dispositional properties would not astonish the man on the street, as far as he understands the term "dispositional property" to mean a property of an object that *may appear* only when some conditions are satisfied. But the man on the street might not know *why* and *how* a dispositional property is being manifested. Such knowledge requires an explanation of the (causal) mechanism bringing about the dispositional effect. One must know e. g. the structure and properties of the chemical compound on the flammable end of the safety-match, as well as the nature of the exothermic chemical reaction, in order to explain the appearance of flame due to a strike, or heat occurring near this end."

This is why in the elaborated BA-theory of time (suggested by L. R. Baker) I had in mind the upper explanation about the way dispositional properties could be manifested. So I proposed a specific relation between a dispositional property of the non-flowing time and human consciousness in order to account for the experience of temporal passage (see section 4.4).[19] However, K. Miller remains silent about the explication of an appropriate counterpart to the introduced dispositional properties, which is in a position to activate their manifestation. This absence, as well as the absence of knowledge about the nature of the introduced dispositional properties,[20] makes her cresting wave theory to remain in the field of the general metaphysical speculations.

Having in mind the last three arguments that are put forward here, I agree with the middle part of the quoted K. Miller's (2018; 26) conclusion that MSTs do not provide a relevant explanation of the phenomenology of temporal passage.

---

[19] One should not draw an analogy between my allegorical expression about the illuminating torch light of consciousness, which attracts two players on the stage of the phenomenology of time passage (the non-flowing time and human consciousness), with the proposed allegory by C. Broad about the policeman's bull's-eye traversing the fronts of the houses in a street, which aims at illustrating the very *movement of presentness* as a fundamental property of time. See (Broad 1923: 59).

[20] In the elaborated BA-theory of time I identified the dispositional property of time for A-properties with the exhibited time asymmetry (see section 4.4).

6.3 The Mind-Dependence of the Passage of Time

The above reached conclusion (see the end of the previous section 6.2) that different versions of the moving spotlight theory do not provide a relevant explanation of the phenomenology of temporal passage was a necessary step here. The reason for the necessity of this step is that these theories have the pretension to solve the problem of temporal passage by accepting *an objective process of a moving presentness*, and thus the debate about the construal of the mind-dependence of temporal passage loses its philosophical significance. But after the above reached conclusion the possibility stays open for an attempt at elucidating the specificity of the mind-dependence of the passage of time; and also for providing arguments in favour of claim (C_6) formulated in section 6.1, which says that the statement about the mind-dependence of the passage of time is not completely equivalent with the statement about its non-existence.

Notwithstanding our experience that time is flowing, i.e. that the present moment (or the moment "now" for any conscious human being) is permanently changing, in the theory of relativity (special and general) there is no place for such a physical process. As a fourth dimension of spacetime time is not flowing.

Following the famous dictum of St. Augustine "What, then, is time? If no one asks me, I know what it is. If I wish to explain it to him who asks me, I do not know",[21] I can resort to a similar avowal:

What is temporal passage? If no one asks me, I know what it is (it is my sense of it). If I wish *to explain it* to him who asks me, I do not know.

Yet I'm convinced that the passage of time is mind-dependent. I have just produced an argument for this conviction: that the theoretical structure of the theory of relativity (special and general) does not include a physical process of a flowing time. And this theory is a well corroborated one, correctly representing the temporal aspect of the physical world. Another argument for this conviction has nothing to do with physical theories. It is the suspicion spurred

---

[21] Confessions, Book eleven, XIV, 17. (Augustin 1955: 183)

on by our rational thinking that time *per se* does not possess an ability to flow.

> If the passage of time requires that time move or flow in anything like the way rivers do then, I think, there is no such thing as the passage of time. If the passage of time requires that we move through time in anything like the way that trains move through space, then there is no such thing as the passage of time. I hold that time is a lot like space, "just another dimension." Of course I think there are differences between the time dimension and the three dimensions of space.[...] *I just deny that there is some mysterious process, "passage," that time undergoes but space does not.* (Skow 2015: 1, my italics)

I express my assent to all that is said by B. Skow in the upper quotation. Time does not really flow, but yet we sense a "mysterious process" of temporal passage, to use his expression. And interesting as it may seem, other authors use similar utterance when speaking about the sense we have for time permanently passing away. As Paul Davies (1995: 283) puts it for instance:

> The overwhelming impression of a flowing, moving time, perhaps acquired through a mental "back door," is a very big mystery.

And also:

> In their search for this mysterious time-flux many scientists have become deeply confused. (Davies 1990: 125)

They are "deeply confused" just in their quality of scientists accepting the theory of relativity, but at the background of their own experience of temporal passage. The latter turns out to be mind-dependent.

Let me make an attempt at analyzing the mysterious phenomenology of temporal passage. I use here the same adjective "mysterious", since if the temporal passage is entirely mind-dependent, it turns out to be an *illusion*. Many B-theorists agree with this assessment, but *this is no consolation for the philosopher seeking the nature of this illusion*. This task, however, proves to be a very hard one.

> According to the B-theory, the passage of time is an
> illusion. The B-theory therefore requires an explana-
> tion of this illusion before it can be regarded as fully
> satisfactory; yet very few B-theorists have taken up the
> challenge of trying to provide one. (Prosser 2012: 93)

A starting point for the demystification of the perception of
flowing time may be rooted in what one means by perceptual experience of movement and change. As I have shown in another
work, however, the interesting suggestions made by Simon Prosser
(2012) and Christoph Hoerl (2013) in this direction fail to fulfill
their aim.[22] What remains then is, as I have mentioned, the nature of the illusion of the passage of time to be elucidated as a
permanent and stubborn subjective phenomenon.

According to claim (C_6) that I am aiming to defend in this
chapter, the statement about the mind-dependence of the passage
of time is not completely equivalent with the statement about its
non-existence.

Well, if the passage of time is a subjective phenomenon that is
compared with an illusion, then *it is not an objective process* presented to our consciousness. And further, if the passage of time is
not an objective process, then it has no objective existence. But is
it true that it possesses no existence whatsoever? To my opinion
the answer to this question is negative, i.e. temporal passage possesses a specific kind of existence, although not an objective, but a
subjective one. And to this effect I can give a preliminary support
to (C_6): the mind-dependence of the passage of time means that
the passage of time lacks an objective existence, but still a subjective existence might be ascribed to it. The latter assertion remains
to be explicated, and this means the illusion of temporal passage
to be elucidated.

So, *what kind of illusion* is the phenomenon of temporal passage? Even those, who firmly support that it is undoubtedly an
illusion, would hardly refer it to the type of illusions already known
to us.

> Does our impression of the flow of time, or the division
> of time into past, present and future, tell us nothing

---

[22]For the defense of this thesis see (Stefanov 2016).

at all about how time is as opposed to how it merely appears to us muddle-headed humans?

As a physicist, I am well aware how much intuition can lead us astray. . . Yet, as a human being, I find it impossible to relinquish the sensation of a flowing time and a moving present moment. It is something so basic to my experience of the world that I am repelled by the claim that it is only an illusion or misperception. It seems to me that there is an aspect of time of great significance that we have so far overlooked in our description of the physical universe. (Davies 1995: 275)

I don't agree with Paul Davies's opinion in the end of the quotation that there is an aspect of time that is both "of great significance," and still "overlooked in our description of the physical universe." But, his heartfelt emotion put aside, Davies is right in saying that as human beings we "find it impossible to relinquish the sensation of a flowing time and a moving present moment." Is this sensation some kind of an illusion? I don't really think so. And I don't think so not because the attempts at elucidating the nature of this illusion have failed so far. I don't think so, because *I don't take the phenomenon of temporal passage to be some kind of an illusion in the ordinary sense of this word.* At most it could be named "illusion" in a figurative sense.

The term "illusion" designates a distortion of one's sensible perception. But always, when we speak of an illusion, we certainly know what feature of a perceived situation is distorted, and probably, *why* it is distorted. Thus for instance we do see a straw inserted into a glass of soda-water to be broken at the liquid surface, but in spite of this we are sure that this is an illusory image. We are sure about this, because if we take out the straw out of the glass, we would see that it is not broken. At that, we have a good explanation for having such an illusion, based on the well-known laws of optical refraction.

Is this the case with the phenomenology of time passage? No, it isn't. Let me remind P. Davies's words that "it is something so basic to my experience of the world that I am repelled by the claim that it is only an illusion or misperception." Contrary to the standard illusion with the broken straw, we are not in a position to draw out time from "the physical universe" just like the straw out of the glass, and see whether it flows, or not. What remains then is making the difference of "how time is as opposed to how it merely appears to us muddle-headed humans." What then is the solution to the steady presence of the alleged illusion?

The initial part of the solution can be formulated as follows:

The phenomenology of time passage is the way in which the physical world is given to us in perceptual experience. To this effect *the flow of time is endowed with empirical reality*, which is provided by the constitution and "working" of human sensibility, or put in the specific transcendental terms, by a pure a priori form of human sensibility. But this formulation is only an entrance to an arguable solution. Resorting to Kant's pure form of sensuous intuition is enough to explain the empirical reality of temporal passage. Indeed, all movements and changes of all objects of experience are perceived, by virtue of our cognitive faculty, to happen in a dynamic tensed series of time.

However, the problem we are facing here is not "Why do we experience time as flowing?" The problem, as we know, is "Why do we have a perceptual experience of time as flowing, while it does not really flow?" This is a problem that has emerged after the introduction of the A-theory and the B-theory of time, and after the acceptance of the latter as more adequate than the former with respect to our contemporary knowledge of space and time in the face of Einstein's theory of relativity. A fundamental concept in this theory is the concept of *spacetime*. Being a dimension of a four-dimensional space, time does not flow, and so our problem arises. The suggested partial solution that the phenomenology of time passage is the way in which the physical world *is given to us* in perceptual experience remains valid of course. What needs a further consideration is the remaining part of the problem: why the physical world is given to us through a phenomenology of passage, if time does not flow?

According to Einstein's special theory of relativity, the persistence of a conscious observer (an individual person) within the four-dimensional spacetime is represented by her world-line. All the events perceived by her are strictly ordered along the world-line satisfying the relations "earlier than" and "later than", as required by the B-theory of time. How then the phenomenology of passage connected with the ever changing moment "now" reins human temporal experience?

The only possible answer to this question is that a continuous series of consecutive regions of three-dimensional subspaces is given to our consciousness at every point along the four-dimensional world-line. But this assumption is exactly the gist of *the elaborated BA-theory of time* presented in section 4.4. It certainly accepts what Hermann Weyl had in mind after realizing the mode of conscious existence of an individual person in spacetime along her definite world-line. Let me here repeat his words:

> The objective world simply *is*, it does not *happen*. Only to the gaze of my consciousness, crawling upward along the life line of my body, does a section of this world come to life as a fleeting image in space which continuously changes in time. (Weyl 1949, 116)

Of course, this is a solution to our problem, but yet an incomplete one. If the solution is not completed it would remain an allegory, maybe a better one, but still an allegory resembling the one exploited by the versions of the moving spotlight theory. A complete solution is provided by the elaborated BA-theory of time. It contains the explication of a dispositional property of time staying at the background of passage phenomenology. This dispositional property is identified with the temporal asymmetry that determines the same direction of three arrows of time – the cosmological one, the thermodynamic one, and the psychological one.

There is no need to repeat my presentation of the elaborated BA-theory to be found in section 4.4. It must be added, however, that if our consciousness "crawling upward along" our world-lines makes "sections of this world to come to life", i.e. if our consciousness makes us to be aware of consecutive three-dimensional slices of spacetime accessible to us, then temporal passage, or the permanent change of the moment "now", turns out to be a basic element of our conscious perception of the world. *The passage of time is not an illusion standardly understood.* Common illusions and even hallucinations are phenomena possessed by human consciousness, but they are temporary wrong presentations and false images, which could badly affect sometimes human life. While the mind-dependent passage of time determines the human way of conscious existence. To remind the words of P. Davies, "it is something so basic to my experience of the world that I am repelled by the claim that it is only an illusion or misperception".

And this conclusion is the reason for the defense of claim (C_6), insisting that the statement about the mind-dependence of the passage of time is not completely equivalent with the statement about the non-existence of the latter. I naturally speak here about *two modes of existence*. The one is objective, ascribed to things as existing in the natural world (independently of the specific way in which they are perceived or described), and to this effect they are not (entirely) mind-dependent. The mode of existence that I ascribe here to the passage of time is a subjective one, but quite different in its uniqueness from the existence of all other subjective perceptions; because it irrevocably goes along with, or to say it better, is interwoven within our human way of conscious existence.

7 DOES TIME FLOW, AT ANY RATE?

Two papers by Claudio Mazzola (2014) and Takeshi Sakon (2016) have recently appeared within the mainstream discussion about the so called passage, or flow of time. Their subject matter is not directed to any concrete A- and B-theories of time staying in opposition, but to offering a resolution to the ongoing debate between the proponents of the two general conceptions: the one which accepts that time is passing in some real manner, and the other one, which insists that time is not flowing, and to this effect "the passage of time" is no more than a metaphorical phrase.

I "borrowed" the title of Mazzola's paper as a heading of this chapter.

> Philosophically unprejudiced language abounds with expressions such as "the flow of time" or "the passage of time", which apparently confer objective dynamical properties on time. Few philosophers are willing to take expressions of this kind literally: they are sometimes called *dynamists*, and their view *dynamism*. The vast majority of philosophers, on the contrary, is reluctant to consider similar expressions anything more than metaphorical characterizations either of the way we experience temporality or of the irreducibility of tensed predication. We may collectively refer to them as the *anti-dynamists*.(. . .) Several philosophers in the analytic tradition, in particular, have argued that phrases such as "time flows" or "time passes" are the result of a category mistake or a semantic shift, to the effect

that time, instead of being conceived as a conceptual or physical precondition of motion, is treated as the subject of motion itself. (Mazzola 2014: 1-2)

Interesting as it may seem, both of the mentioned authors raise the claim that the so called *no-rate argument*,[23] having the pretension to ascertain that time does not flow, because time flux has no well-defined rate or speed, *cannot fulfil its aim*. Mazzola and Sakon maintain that *time could still be accepted to flow, but without a well-defined rate*. Thus the claim that time is literally flowing can be saved.

In contrast to their view, I'll try to defend in this chapter the following claim:

(C_7) The view that time flows literally without a well-defined rate exhibits conceptual flaws.

Anti-dynamists, being "the vast majority of philosophers", or not, stick to the no-rate argument, because consistently developed, it leads to the conclusion that time does not literally flow. The argument as presented extendedly by Mazzola (2014: 2-3) runs to the following:

(1) Time flows literally.

(2) If time flows literally, it flows at a well-defined rate.

(3) If time flows at a well-defined rate, that rate is one second per second.

(4) One second per second is one.

(5) One is an adimensional number.

(6) No adimensional number is a well-defined rate.

It is easily seen, however, that premises (3)–(6) lead to the claim that time does not flow at a well-defined rate. And in so far as premise (2) is uncontroversial (at least for the anti-dynamists), then (2)–(6) entail the conclusion that statement (1) is wrong, i.e. that *time does not flow literally*.

Well, but dynamists struggle to evade this conclusion. In order this to be done some of the premises that constitute the no-rate argument must be rejected as unacceptable. Premises (3) and (4)

---

[23] For the same argument Takeshi Sakon (2016) uses the name "rate-argument".

have usually attracted attempts at rejection, but these attempts have proved not to be convincing. This is why Mazzola directs his criticism to premise (2). This is a good strategy for a dynamist, because if it turned out to be successful, i.e. if (2) could be shown to be false, the unwanted conclusion would certainly fail.

Premise (2) is neither semantically false, nor strange as insistence. If time flows literally, it could eventually flow at a well-defined rate. But as we have seen, this is no good assumption for the dynamists. Only one possibility remains then: premise (2) to be rejected by the claim that *time flows literally, but without a well-defined rate*. And this is the claim that Mazzola tries to defend in his paper.

He begins by the elucidation of the notion of motion. If something flows (as time is accepted to do) it is undoubtedly in motion, so we must work with a rational *theory of motion*. Mazzola (2014: 5) is sticking to the standard theory, known as the "*at-at* theory of motion". According to it an object is in motion, only when it is observed to be found *at different places in space at different times*. The at-at theory has a simple formal presentation, on the base of the Cartesian product of three sets: $X \times S \times T$, where X denotes the set of moving objects, S – the set of spatial positions $\{s_1, s_2, \dots \}$, and T – the set of moments of time during the motion of an object $\{t_1, t_2, \dots \}$. Then the ordered triples (x, s_1, t_1) and (x, s_2, t_2) belonging to the Cartesian product represent the motion of the object $x \subset X$, only when s_1 and s_2, and t_1 and t_2 are pair-wise different.

Let us now turn our attention to time. Can we say that the at-at theory of motion could be used to describe the motion of time? No, we cannot. Because even if we were dynamists, we should find it meaningless to say that time is here or there within space at different moments of time. Time helps us to ascertain whether a physical object is moving through space, but time is not by itself a subject of motion. This is the reason for Mazzola to suggest another theory to describe time's motion, called by him "an extended theory of motion". Let me now adduce a longer quotation in the words of which the content of his extended theory is exposed. As it seems, the attribute "extended" is added only because the theory is contended to be applicable to the way time is moving, while still keeping it as an independent variable.

Premise (3) claims that, if time moves at a well-defined rate, that rate must be one second per second. Rates of passage or motion are ordinarily measured in units of the dependent variable of motion per units of its independent variable. So, according to premise (3), the dependent variable of the motion of time must be measured in seconds. *Since seconds are units of duration, it follows that the dependent variable of the motion of time must coincide with time itself.* This means that, according to premise (3), time moves by being at different times at different times.(...) (my italics)

Premise (3) thus requires that time could take over the role of space in the at-at theory of motion. More exactly, the physical space S should be replaced by a wider space consisting in the union of S and T, where T is supposed to denote time, exactly as before. Ordinary motions are accordingly analysed in the usual way, while the motion of time is analysed in terms of (pairs of) ordered triples whose elements are, in order, time (taken as a mover), a time (taken as a position), and a time (taken as the time at which time, understood as the mover, is in that position).

Let us call this the *extended at-at theory of motion*. Contrary to the at-at theory, this analysis of motion is *prima facie* compatible with dynamism. As a further proof of this, consider the claim, frequently made by the dynamists, that time flows *from* past *to* future: according to this claim, time traces a trajectory within itself, as it were, precisely as requested by the extended at-at theory. (Ibid: 6-7)

I don't find this exposition of the extended at-at theory of motion to be consistent. I may not be right, but I can really hardly grasp the meaning of some declarations that are present in the "extended" quotation. The contention from the first part of the quotation that time by itself as duration is a "dependent variable", which is dependent *on itself* as an independent variable, so that "time moves by being at different times at different times", is no more than a curious enigma.

The second part of the quotation is an additional formal description of what has been already said in the first part. "The union of S and T, where T is supposed to denote time, exactly as before" is postulated to be a global space containing the time positions occupied by the moving time itself. Thus time is taken once to be a mover, twice as a "spatial" position, and thrice as an indicating time of its own motion. It comes out that the moving time is at a place in "spatial" time, and at a time in itself.

The third part of the quotation insists that a "further proof" of the extended at-at theory of motion is "the claim, frequently made by the dynamists, that time flows *from* past *to* future: according to this claim, time traces a trajectory within itself, as it were, precisely as requested by the extended at-at theory." I don't see how the claim that time flows from past to future (the incomprehensible declaration that "time traces a trajectory within itself" notwithstanding) could be taken as a *proof* of the extended at-at theory of motion, if it is exactly the time flux that has to be demonstrated through this theory, and not vice versa.

All these comments clearly show that Mazzola's extended at-at theory of motion could hardly be taken as a consistent ontological model representing the flow (the movement) of time.

The exposition of the extended at-at theory of motion does not yet solve the problem "Does time flow at some rate, or not?" For this purpose Mazzola turns his attention to elucidate the concept of speed[24] in the description of motion, in order to overthrow premise (2). This is his central aim, since "The no-raters [the proponents of the no-rate argument] might contend that premise (2) is self-evident because the concept of motion analytically presupposes the concept of speed" (Ibid: 8). So, he makes an attempt to show "that the physical conception of speed is not analytically presupposed by the physical idea of motion" (Ibid).

My claim is that he has not fulfilled his aim. Of course, generally speaking, his last statement is correct. The at-at theory of

---

[24] The concept of speed is usually understood as the magnitude of the velocity of a moving object, so I am not sure why Mazzola works with this concept, rather than with the concept of velocity. Probably the reason for this is that he takes for granted that time has only one and unalterable direction. We know that according to him "time flows from past to future". This is not true, however, for material objects being in motion. And this is not a side-issue, in so far as he deals with a theory of motion in general.

motion is sufficient to define the physical idea of motion. It is not necessary for one to know the exact values of speeds exhibited by a moving body in order to say that there is a real motion going on. Very few people know for instance the speed of the Moon revolution around the Earth, but hardly anybody would deny that the Moon is moving around our planet. Knowledge of its linear and angular velocity relative to the Earth is not needed for knowing that the Moon is moving, but this knowledge is indispensable for the exact description of the motion of the natural satellite around the Earth. To this effect I can say that yes, "the physical conception of speed is not analytically presupposed by the physical idea of motion", but the concept of speed must be presupposed for the general *idea* of motion *to be specified for every case of motion*, so that a complete mechanical picture could be presented of it.

Mazzola embraces further the stipulation that he has in mind not the concept of speed at a time (of instantaneous speed), but the concept of *average speed*:

> [W]e shall concentrate on the idea of average speed, namely the displacement or increment of the spatial variable per unit of time. This choice is motivated by three reasons. Firstly, it will allow us not to rule out a priori non-continuous models of time, because the idea of instantaneous speed is inextricably associated with the assumption that time is continuous. Secondly, it will help us avoid bothersome and irrelevant complications concerning the infinite derivability of the equations of motion. Finally, it will allow us not to get involved in the tangled issue whether or not moving objects should necessarily possess a well-defined speed at each time. (Ibid: 9)

However, this stipulation distorts his analysis just along the pointed reasons for his motivation. Why Mazzola would like to "rule out a priori non-continuous models of time"? The standard concept of instantaneous speed in classical physics is introduced as the first-order derivative of the position in space with respect to time.[25] This means that time is traditionally accepted to be

---

[25] This is rather the definition of velocity, but can be adjusted for speed as well, see previous f. 24.

continuous, while Mazzola includes non-continuous models of time as well. I assume that he makes this step for the sake of achieving his aim: to show that time flows without a well-defined rate. But discontinuous models of time distort the classical concept of speed, which Mazzola wants to discredit. And also, if he accepts that time is discontinuous, this would certainly affect his previous contentions of the kind that "time moves by being at different times at different times", at least because the separate time moments have to be in constant correlation, which is an additional *ad hoc* hypothesis.

His second reason is trivial, so let me look at the third one. It is the exhortation that having in mind only average speed we will not be involved "in the tangled issue whether or not moving objects should necessarily possess a well-defined speed at each time." As it seems, this reason attracts superfluous generality concerning the way in which objects could be "principally" in motion. It is well known that moving objects do possess average speed, but only because it can be calculated on the base of their instantaneous speeds in the course of their specific motions. I don't know a single case of a classical object (time flow being left aside) that can really move with no well-defined speed.

So, it comes out that Mazzola's stipulation *is not a cogent part of an argument*. But he turns also to an additional story in support of his declaration "that the physical conception of speed is not analytically presupposed by the physical idea of motion":

> If the concept of speed was analytically presupposed by the concept of motion, then one could not in principle grasp the concept of motion in a full and adequate way, without also understanding the notion of speed, namely the measure of displacement per unit of time. But then it would follow that, by the same token, one could not in principle fully understand the idea of speed without also understanding the idea of acceleration, namely the increment of speed per unit of time. Similarly, if that was the case, then the concept of acceleration would similarly presuppose the concept of jerk, i.e. the increment of acceleration per unit of time. Evidently, one could proceed this way without end; but then, due to the chain of implications, the concept of motion would turn out to presuppose infinitely many concepts, thereby be-

coming indeterminate.(...) To preserve the idea of motion from such an unjust fate, we must conclude that the idea of motion does not analytically presuppose the concept of speed in the first place.

Let us call this the *conceptual regression argument...* (Ibid: 9-10)

Does Mazzola's conceptual regression argument hold water? No, it does not.

It is trivially true, of course, that if the first contention of the adduced argument were correct, the whole argument then would come out to be correct on the base of the undertaken regression. The problem here is with the content of the first contention, which I find to be unacceptable. And if this is the case, the regression fails to fulfil its aim as a regression *ad infinitum*, since *its first premise is false.* Why is this the case?

The first premise is telling us that "one could not in principle grasp the concept of motion in a full and adequate way, without also understanding the notion of speed, namely the measure of displacement per unit of time". And since one cannot grasp the idea of motion without the concept of the measure of displacement per unit of time, this concept is analytically presupposed by the concept of motion.

This reasoning is flawed because of two facts. They have been already mentioned, so I shall briefly repeat them. The first fact is that the concept of displacement per unit of time, i.e. the concept of average speed is dependent on the concept of instantaneous speed, since the former concept is the average value of the instantaneous speeds over the trajectory of a moving object. The second fact is, as I have pointed out, that grasping the idea of motion *does not* presuppose the concept of speed, despite that it is necessary for every case of motion to be specified and completely described. Thus the untenability of the first premise leads to the untenability of the whole conceptual regression argument. This eliminates Mazzola's conviction that the standard definition of motion allegedly presupposes the concept of speed.

It is seen that Mazzola's argumentation fails up to now to be a sound prerequisite for supporting his claim that time flows literally without a well-defined rate. However, he continues with his effort by insisting that "the variation-rate hypothesis, is logically incompatible with the premises of the no-rate argument. Hence, the no-raters cannot consistently rely on it in order to defend premise (2)" (Ibid: 12). "No-raters", as we already know, are the proponents of the no-rate argument. But what is "the variation-rate hypothesis"? It is the hypothesis that "every variation of a scalar quantity with respect to time is a rate" (Ibid). This hypothesis is acceptable as a general statement. But why the variation-rate hypothesis is logically incompatible with the premises of the no-rate argument, so that no-raters cannot rely on it in order to defend premise (2)?

> To understand why, let us first recall that the no-raters must provisionally concede the adequacy of the extended at-at theory, which is implied by premise (3). Thus they must concede, albeit only for the sake of their reductio, that time can literally move by being at different times at different times, and notably that time covers a distance of one second in an interval of one second. Hence, they must agree that time undergoes a genuine form of quantitative change, that such a change consists in the variation of a temporal quantity with respect to a temporal quantity, and that the value of that variation is one second per second. Now, given the variation-rate hypothesis, this variation should necessarily constitute a rate. However, this result would openly contradict premises (4)–(6), according to which one second per second is one and hence not a rate at all. To summarise: given premise (3), and hence given the extended at-at theory of motion, premises (4)–(6) become incompatible with the variation-rate hypothesis. (Ibid: 12)

This quotation contains a misunderstanding to the effect that "the no-raters must provisionally concede the adequacy of the extended at-at theory, which is implied by premise (3)". First, the extended at-at theory is Mazzola's suggestion, and is not necessarily implied by premise (3). And second, as I have already shown, Mazzola's extended at-at theory is untenable. One could hardly maintain that time is moving "by being at different times at different times" as a realization of a real physical process.

This misunderstanding left aside, let us agree that premises (4)–(6) are incompatible with the variation-rate hypothesis, so that no-raters cannot rely on it in order to defend premise (2). But there is an argumentative trap here in relation to the variation-rate hypothesis. It states that "every variation of a scalar quantity with respect to time is a rate". If time flows literally, then its flux is the variation of a temporal quantity with respect to a temporal quantity, and so, according to the variation-rate hypothesis, this variation should necessarily constitute a rate. This contention is acknowledged in the adduced quotation, but it stays in harmony with premise (2) stating that if time flows literally, it flows at a well-defined rate.

The only exit left for the dynamists to rebut premise (2) is the general character of the variation-rate hypothesis to be examined and cancelled. According to this hypothesis, a space mover displays certainly a well-defined speed, because its motion is characterized by a variation of a scalar quantity with respect to time. Within the framework of the extended at-at theory of motion, however, the variation-rate hypothesis loses its general strength, because a second requirement for a mover to possess a well-defined rate of motion is not fulfilled. This is the requirement the dependent and the independent variable that undergo an increment during the variation (the process of motion) to be not of one and the same quality. Time is exactly the example of breaking this requirement, because the time flux is represented by the variation of a temporal quantity with respect to a temporal quantity, and so both variables have one and the same quality. Mazzola thus reaches the conclusion that

> Within the extended at-at theory of motion, then, it is perfectly legitimate to admit that some mover, notably all the movers whose dependent variable is time, can move without speed. (Ibid: 14)

In the end it comes out that what Mazzola has tried to assert is no more than a mere conceptual replacement. Anti-dynamists infer from premise (3) of the no-rate argument that (4) and (5) are valid statements. While Mazzola installs premise (3) in the context of his extended at-at theory of motion and insists that this construal leads to the conclusion that time flows without a well-defined rate. So, the bone of contention comes out to be the extended at-at theory of motion. If it is an untenable theory of motion, and I maintain that it is, then Mazzola has not achieved his aim to demonstrate that time flows without a well-defined rate.

This conclusion undoubtedly supports claim (C_7) from the beginning of this chapter, stating that the view that time flows literally without a well-defined rate exhibits conceptual flaws.

Now let me turn to Takeshi Sakon's position on temporal flow, which is parallel to Mazzola's one. And let me remind that the no-rate argument is re-named by T. Sakon (2016: 471) as "rate argument against the passage of time" (see fn. 22).

Roughly speaking, the argument runs as follows: (i) if time passes, its passage must occur at some rate, but (ii) there is no such rate; hence, the passage of time is a myth. (Ibid)

No doubt, Sakon's attempt is directed to the rejection of claim (ii). In his words:

> The question of how fast time passes has intrigued many people because it appears that there is a strong conceptual connection between time passing and its passing at some rate.(...) *The main purpose of the current paper is to break such a conceptual link.* Success in this attemp will not only provide us with a reason for rejecting the rate argument but will also shed some light on the nature of time. If I am correct in saying that time may pass with or without a rate, it will mean that the rate argument, which rests upon the very question of how fast time passes, is irrelevant to the debate between the dynamic view of time (the view that time passes in some sense) and the static view of time (the view that time does not pass in any sense). It is then far from trivial to see that the passage of time (at least in its essence) need not involve the notion of rate. (Sakon 2016: 472, my italics)

But how the passage of time could be interpreted? According to Sakon there are two ways for this. The one is to identify temporal passage with changes in things, which is dubbed by the author "the Priorian passage theory". The other way is the view that the passage of time is something more than or independent of changes in things, and is dubbed "the pure passage theory" (Sakon 2016: 472-473). The thesis that is further defended is that both of these theories are immune to the rate argument.

Why the Priorian passage theory according to Sakon is immune to the rate argument? The given answer is very simple and *prima facie* convincing. Even though the passage of time could be assessed as a metaphor, it is evinced in the observable changes of the properties of things. The poker was hot an hour ago, but now it is cold, or it is hot now, but will be cold in an hour. The passage of time is nothing else but (is expressed by) the real changes of things and to this effect the question whether it has a rate or not is irrelevant in the framework of this theory. To be more explicit Sakon gives an imaginary example. Let us suppose that the whole universe becomes stationary with the exception of one solitary working clock. Its big hand is moving, and it covers one second per second. It doesn't matter whether this ratio is interpreted as a rate or not. If there is a change in the movement of the clock's hand, then time passes with, or without a well-defined rate. So, the conclusion is being reached that "if the passage of time consists in changes in things, whether its passage has a rate is irrelevant in determining its existence" (Ibid: 477). Thus one can maintain that, in so far as "the passage of time (at least in its essence) need not involve the notion of rate" (see the end of the quotation), the passage of time exhibits no well-defined rate.

It is easily seen that Sakon's argumentation concerning the so called Priorian passage theory is based on ordinary "everyday" examples of changes in things. At the background of these examples his conclusion may seem to be correct. His conclusion fails, however, if a well confirmed consequence from the theory of relativity is taken into account. It states that one and the same changes in the properties of things depend on the character of motion of the reference frame in which they occur, as well as on the strength of the gravitation nearby. Thus Sakon's solitary clock will not be equally working within different frames of reference. The well-known clocks paradox or twins paradox suffices to be mentioned here. The clock of the brother twin who has travelled away from the Earth to come back again to meet his brother on Earth would show less elapse of time, so that he would be younger than his brother. But if one and the same clock, solitary or not, works differently in different frames of reference, then it is quite meaningful to be acknowledged that its hand is moving with a different rate in accordance with its "situation" in the universe. Hence the concept of rate cannot be excluded from the passage of time, if the latter is construed as the change of things.

So, it comes out that the Priorian passage theory is not immune to the rate argument as Sakon has tried to convince us.

But this is not the end of Sakon's attempt at surmounting the rate argument:

> Those dissatisfied with the Priorian passage theory may instead be attracted to the view that, among various changes, there should be a special kind of change called *pure passage*, which is something more than or independent of changes in things. Note that just positing the independent temporal dimension does not imply the existence of pure passage. It should also have a dynamic aspect: time really passes or flows in some sense.(...) Let us call this view the 'pure passage theory'. (Ibid: 478-479)

At the very outset I want to point here to a claim that is tacitly postulated, and which is then aimed at as a result of analysis. The claim is: "*time really passes or flows in some sense*". If one has in mind this tacit assumption, then she may go on with the reasoning undertaken by Sakon. And it is the following. If the rate of change of an arbitrary process must be measured we need to use a periodic process as a basic standard expressed for instance by the movement of clock's hands, the positions of the sun, and the like. But such a measurement is possible only because there is a pure passage of time.

> When we compare the rate of a physical change to that of the change in the position of the hands on our clock or of the sun, in reality we intend to measure the rate of change in terms of pure passage, *even though beings like us do not perceive it directly*. We just assume that our clock or the sun is a fairly good stand-in for pure passage.(...) (Ibid: 480, my italics)

So, the assumption is that there is a pure passage of time, which is not directly perceivable for us as human beings, but for which periodic processes can be considered as its representations. Of course, real clocks could work well or bad, by displaying defects in measuring the time, if they work faster or slower. However, if we imagine a "clock" measuring the pure time, it would certainly be a unique standard for how time is passing *per se*. Then unlike the real clocks around us the imaginary clock would necessarily measure one hour when just one hour has passed. Pure time passes at the rate of one hour per hour.

> If so, the question of how fast time passes is no more sensible to ask than how long one metre is. The answers to both questions are instances of the necessary a priori and are therefore tautological or meaningless in the sense that they cannot be false.(...) (Ibid: 484)

The clear answers are that one meter is always one meter, and that one hour is always one hour. To this effect if one asks the question "how fast does pure time pass?" she would receive the answer that time passes one hour per hour. This is the rate of pure passage to itself. *And since the question presupposes a tautological answer, this is not a sensible question.* "Defenders of the pure passage theory may simply respond that the rate argument poses a nonsense question that need not be answered" (Ibid: 485). Thus the rate argument can be relinquished on this ground. And in so far as the aim of its proponents is reaching the conclusion that time does not pass literally, Sakon adheres to the following specification:

> The rate argument is driven by the question of how fast time passes, but fails to defeat the idea that time passes, because time may pass even if we cannot ask its rate meaningfully. (Ibid: 487)

However, I state that the pure passage theory is not in a position to reject the rate argument against the passage of time. I can point to *two reasons* in support of my statement.

The first one I have already mentioned at the beginning of the presentation of the pure passage theory. In the whole course of their analysis its proponents *presuppose* that there is something as pure time, that is to say that there is time, which is independent of the concrete development of all physical processes, and which passes in some sense. Periodical motions occurring in nature cannot principally explicate whether pure time passes with some rate or not, but their mutual rates do clearly show that pure time passes literally. However, it is evident that *the pure passage theory is based on a circular reasoning*. Its proponents tacitly assume the dynamic reality of a pure time, i.e. they take for granted that pure time is a flowing time *per se*, and then by attracting the periodical motions of some physical processes contend that the passage of pure time is evinced through them, although the question "how fast does pure time pass?" is meaningless.

The second reason is closely related to the first one. Let me remind Sakon's conviction that there is a pure passage of time, which is not directly perceivable for us as human beings, but for which periodic processes can be considered as its representations. Thus it comes out that although the pure passage theory is different from the previously considered Priorian passage theory (because it presupposes pure time, while the Priorian theory has no need of it), it also relies for its exposition on the secondary help of physical periodic process. If they were not present in nature, they could not be taken as representations of pure time's passage.

On the base of these two reasons I can conclude that the pure passage theory, like the Priorian passage theory, cannot provide a counter-argument against the (no-) rate argument.

This conclusion lends further support to claim (C_7) from the beginning of this chapter, stating that the view that time flows literally without a well-defined rate exhibits conceptual flaws.

*

Although that I am not a dynamist, I have some sympathy for the attempts of Claudio Mazzola and Takeshi Sakon to defend the possibility for time to flow without a well-defined rate. If they were successful in their attempts, the no-rate argument might be overcome; and by this the negation of the statement that time flows literally could be rejected. Namely this is the central aim of the two authors: to defend dynamism (the dynamic conception of time). In spite of my criticism, my sympathy goes with the conditional statement that if their analyses were correct, then we should have the possibility to accept that time flows in some way, and thus to be happy that our awareness of this corresponds to the real temporal feature of the world.

However, the world has proved to be more complex than the picture of it drawn by our immediate empirical experience. Let me remind here Brian Greene's avowal from the beginning of section 2.2 that "when it comes to revealing the true nature of reality, common experience is deceptive" (Greene 2011: 5). And also:

> The overarching lesson that has emerged from scientific inquiry over the last century is that human experience is often a misleading guide to the true nature of reality. Lying just beneath the surface of the everyday is a world we'd hardly recognize. (Greene 2004: 5)

Bradford Skow has also made an attempt at saving the moving spotlight theories[26] from the grip of the no-rate argument, probably lead by the same wishful consideration. He writes that

> (1) If something moves, it moves with some determinate velocity. The question "How fast does it move?" is a meaningful question.

> (2) If the moving spotlight theory is true then presentness moves (along the series of times). (Skow 2015: 104)

Well, but if it is acknowledged that presentness moves literally, then it must do so with some determinate velocity, according to clause (1). But can one determine the velocity of the moving presentness? In order to evade the answer to this question B. Skow questions the veracity of clause (1).

> Is the analogue of (1) true about all change? Is it true that if something changes, it must change at some definite rate? Certainly not. Consider George. During his adventures in the city George got hungrier and hungrier. Must he have been getting hungrier at some determinate rate? Is it sensible to ask, precisely how fast was his hunger increasing? No. (Ibid)

But I can ask, on my side, is the comparison between the dynamic of George's getting hungrier and hungrier and the movement of time's presentness a correct one. *I say no.* Even if Skow is right to insist that clause (1) is not true for all kinds of change, it is undoubtedly true for those changes whose increments (increases and

---

[26] About the moving spotlight theories see section 6.2.

decreases) are measurable. And the alleged movement of presentness is exactly of this kind, if it must be construed as a movement
in the literal sense of the word. Hence Skow could hardly overcome
the requirement of clause (1) in relation to the moving spotlight
theories pretending that time's presentness is really moving.

As I have already presumed, Skow's attempt at saving the moving spotlight theories from the grip of the no-rate argument is directed by the same wishful consideration as mine is. This is the
acknowledgment that the moving spotlight theories stay closer to
our sense experience of a flowing time than the eternalist position
of the anti-dynamists. The reason for my presumption I see in the
final words of his *Introduction*:

> I think that the endgame in the debate between the
> block universe theory and the moving spotlight theory
> is over how the theories make sense of our experience
> of time. I think that the strongest case in favor of the
> moving spotlight theory starts with the claim that it
> explains some features of our experience better than
> the block universe does. (Ibid; 3)

However, even if Skow's observation is true, it gives no argument about which of the two theories represent in a better way the
temporal feature of the natural world. Because, following Brian
Greene's advice, one must concede that "The overarching lesson
that has emerged from scientific inquiry over the last century is
that human experience is often a misleading guide to the true nature of reality."

Our experience may prove to be misleading about how physical
reality is structured. And we need an additional investigation to
realize that sometimes our direct experience is misleading, and why
this is so. Having this in mind I proposed the elaborated BA-theory
of time (in section 4.4) to account for how time seems to be flowing,
if it does not do so.

8 THE RELATIONALIST-SUBSTANTIVALIST DEBATE

8.1 Preliminary Words

Since the Newton-Leibniz debate about the substantival or the relational nature of space and time the problem is still a bone of contention among philosophers. The so called "relationalist-substantivalist debate" continues to focus on itself the non-fading interest of philosophers, merely because of the (conceptual as well as practical) necessity for grasping the nature of space and time; and because "science is still struggling to understand what space and time actually are" (Greene 2004: IX).

I shall not be concerned with historical facts of the debate. My aim here is to develop three basic arguments in support of the substantival view. The first one is a critical assessment of the classical shift argument and the so called void argument, the second one relies on the exhibition of properties of spacetime as an entity, and the third argument comes from a consistent interpretation of Einstein's equation, basic for the theory of general relativity. To this effect the claim that I shall argue for in this chapter is:

(C$_8$) In the relationalist-substantivalist debate preference has to be given to the substantival nature of spacetime.

According to the substantival view classical Newtonian space and time, as well as spacetime within the ontology of general relativity, are autonomous entities having an existence of their own, and thus being independent of the way of existence of material objects and fields. On the contrary, according to the relational view, only material objects and fields really exist, while space and time are nothing else but the spatial and temporal relations among them. My arguments in favour of substantivalism will not involve mathematical language, e.g. formal transformations of spacetime metrical structures, with the exception of a well-known equation from the theory of general relativity within the fourth section of this chapter. The arguments are predominantly of a conceptual nature.

In the next section 8.2 I expose a counter-argument to Leibniz's shift argument. The latter has the pretension to convincingly ascertain the relational nature of classical space. Then to the extent to which the counter-argument fulfils its task, it could be seen as an implicit argument in support of the substantival nature of space. I then present an additional argument supporting the relational character of space, which I dub "the void argument" , and show that its pretention has to be also rejected.

In sections 8.3 I raise and analyze the statement that if spacetime were relational, not substantival, then it couldn't possess nonrelational properties, which spacetime really exhibits. I mean here the re-introduction of the cosmological constant, and the recent detection of gravitational waves.

In section 8.4 another thesis is proposed in support of the fundamental nature of space-time, involving a consistent interpretation of the basic equation in the general theory of relativity.

If the arguments from sections 8.2 – 8.4 do hold water, they lend a strong support to claim (C_8) about the substantival nature of spacetime.

8.2 Leibniz's Shift Argument Revisited. The Void Argument

Leibniz's famous objection against Newton's substantival conception of physical space is his so called "shift argument" . This argument was elaborated later, using the mathematical language of general relativity, with the aim to demonstrate the relational character of spacetime, and is known by the name of the "hole argument". I'll not touch upon it, since it presupposes some formal considerations concerning diffeomorphic transformations of the metric tensor field[27] of Riemannian spacetime, while my analysis remains at the level of ideas.[28] To this effect I am going to analyze the initial premise of Leibniz's shift argument. Instead of re-telling the argument by myself, I set out here its clear presentation made by Frank Arntzenius (2012: 126):

> Leibniz, the continental rival of Newton, gave a famous argument against the existence of space. His argument was as follows. Suppose that space did in fact exist. Now (...) imagine a universe that is exactly the same as ours, except that every material object, throughout the history of that universe, is shifted to a different location in space. Say, every material object is shifted 5 feet in the direction that the Eiffel tower now points. Such a universe would not differ in any discernible way from the actual universe. Therefore, God could have had no reason to create our universe rather than such a shifted universe. But God has a reason for everything he does. So it cannot be that there is such a choice to be made. Now, if there is no space, if all that exists is material objects, which stand in certain distance relations, then there is no such choice to be made. For, all the distance relations between material objects are the same in the actual universe and in the shifted universe. Thus, if all that exists is material objects, which stand in distant relations to one another, then there are no such two distinct possibilities, and thus there is no choice for God to make...
>
> Shorn of religious zeal, the argument boils down to this. If space exists, there is a difference between a universe and a shifted universe. But that is a difference without a difference. And why introduce such an elusive difference if you do not need it? Leibniz concluded that space does not exist – that there are only bits of matter which stand in spatial (distance) relations.

---

[27] It is usually called a "tensor field" in this argument to the extent to which it steps in a kind of equality with the tensor of matter – see section 8.4.

[28] All the more that a critical attitude to the "hole argument" is already present in contemporary literature. See for instance Arntzenius 2012: 139-141.

Leibniz's shift argument seems to be convincing. It is easily seen that it relies on the well-known principle of the identity of indiscernibles, and I am not going to contest the applicability of this principle. Nevertheless, I'll try to develop a counter-argument. As being a counter-argument to the shift argument, it is at the same time an implicit argument in support of the substantival view of space. It aims at elucidating the dubious role of the initial premise of Leibniz's argument, that is to say, *the presupposition for a spatial shift*. This presupposition can be interpreted in two different ways, depending on the understanding of how the assumed shift is possible.

The first possible way is to admit the existence of a Newtonian absolute space, as well as the principal possibility of shifting material objects through space. Thus the entire system of worldwide objects together with their interactions could hypothetically be shifted by a finite distance away from their actual place in space, so that during the translation process until its end all material objects and their interactions remain identical to themselves. The problem that I see here is that this initial presupposition already conceals the very conclusion of the shift argument. Just admit the existence of absolute space, which "invites" any shifts of material objects within it, and you'll reach the intended conclusion that no absolute space exists. However, the only conclusion that could really be made within this interpretation of the shift argument (by the help of the principle of the identity of indiscernibles) is the conclusion about the one-ness, or in other words, about *the uniqueness of the universe*, and not directly about the non-existence of space.

Let me turn now to the second possible construal of the initial premise of the shift argument, i.e. of the very presupposition for a spatial shift. Here again the talk of two allegedly different universes comes to the fore: the actual one, and another one, which is the result of the shift of the former carried out at a finite distance. The difference now is that each universe is taken initially to be situated within its own space. But if so, then a super-space is needed, in order for a universe to be shifted to another region of it. Though being identical with the actual universe, the other one occupies another region of super-space, which encompasses the two spatial universes. In this case the shift argument can be used to reject the existence of super-space, but not for reaching the sought conclusion about the non-existence of space at all – the space of the actual (and unique) universe.

So, by exploring the two possibilities about how the spatial shift of the whole universe could be construed, it comes out that the shift argument is not a cogent argument against the substantival nature of space.

Yet a follower of Leibniz may relinquish the shift argument and replace it with another one, which can be called the "*void argument*". It runs to the following:

"Let us assume that besides all material objects and fields in the world there is space in which all of them are situated, and that space is *something* that has a reality of its own. Now let us imagine that all material objects and fields are taken away. What would remain then is the presupposed universal space. But this empty space would then be only a void deprived of material objects and interactions among them, and to this effect it would turn into an imaginary thing, which displays no property of its own. But a thing without properties whatsoever is rather nothing than something. However, God created the world *as something*, not as nothingness. This is why space does not exist as an entity of its own. It is an idea that emerges through *the reification of the entire set of relations* among material objects."

A strong objection to the void argument would be a claim that an empty space is not deprived of intrinsic qualities. Let us turn to this effect to the concept of a triangle. The sum of the inner angles of every triangle drawn on a plane equals 180 degrees. However, if the triangle is to be found on the surface of a sphere, the sum of its inner angles is more than 180 degrees. Thus basic properties of triangles may differ, when they reside within different spaces. And this difference is not due to the triangles proper, but due to a difference of the spaces themselves. A geometrical space can be flat, or otherwise can have positive or negative curvature, a space can possess homogeneous or non-homogeneous metric, spaces can exhibit different topologies, for instance they can be orientable, or non-orientable. All of these properties are properties of a geometrical space *per se*, so every space is characterized by a list of the aforementioned qualities. On these grounds the claim that an empty space has qualities of its own must be avowed to be true, and hence it follows that space may be viewed as an entity of its own.

Of course, an objection may be raised that the qualities of a geometrical space just pointed out, do support a view about some ideal autonomy of geometrical spaces, but not the stronger thesis about the substantival character of an empty physical space (spacetime).

I agree with this objection; but I have also a straightforward answer to it. And it is the following: if an entity different from the material objects can affect their behavior, then it could be taken as certain that such an entity is substantial. And as it is well known, it is the curvature of the four-dimensional spacetime that is said to affect the motion of material bodies, as well as of the light beams passing near massive cosmic objects.

A counter-objection may be raised that my criticism of the void argument, even if taken to be sound in some sense, still does not hold water. And this is so, because from a historical point of view non-Euclidean geometries were (probably) unknown to Leibniz. I do step here into a delicate argumentative field.

I must confess that if one presumes that what is taken to be *the* physical space is correctly represented geometrically by the flat three-dimensional Euclidean space, then the void argument might go well. And this was the undoubted presumption at the time of the Newton – Leibniz debate. However, this same argument does not work nowadays. As it was already mentioned, light beams are not straight lines near the boundaries of massive cosmic objects. And this is so, because of the Riemannian character of spacetime. The geometrical feature of a space to be either flat, or to possess a kind of curvature, can affect the motion of material objects. Thus the void argument may well be rejected.

8.3   Properties of Spacetime as an Entity

If spacetime were relational, then it couldn't possess non-relational properties, which are accepted to be possessed as properties by *material systems*. But it is known today that spacetime really exhibits such properties. Let me start with the fact that a specific kind of "internal" energy, under the popular name of "dark energy", is ascribed to spacetime.

When A. Einstein firstly wrote his equation of the general theory of relativity, he introduced an additional term, known as the cosmological constant, so that the equation could describe a static Universe. When astronomic observations showed that this was not the case, he removed this term. However, 43 years after Einstein was gone, observations showed not only that the Universe is expanding, but also that its expansion is accelerating. Contemporary cosmologists looked back at Einstein's cosmological constant. They have done this for the sake of a cogent explanation for the observed acceleration of the expansion of the Universe. And even if this acceleration would not be confirmed by interpreting new astrophysical observational data, the universal expansion is an established fact, and it is certainly in need of an explanation.

As well as matter, the universe may contain what is called "vacuum energy", energy that is present even in apparently empty space... vacuum energy causes the expansion to accelerate, as in inflation. In fact, vacuum energy acts just like the cosmological constant... that Einstein added to his original equations in 1917, when he realized that they didn't admit a solution representing a static universe. (Hawking 2001, pp. 96-97)

The energy ruling the expansion of the Universe is something that cosmologists refer to the "empty" spacetime itself. Dark energy opposes the effect of mutual attraction among stars and galaxies due to the universal gravitation. The gravitational force is inversely proportional to the square of the distances among material bodies, so this interaction becomes weaker in an expanding space pushing material configurations aside from each other. However, if dark energy expressed by the cosmological constant is a quality of spacetime as such, its anti-gravitational effect ought to be one and the same independently of the fact how much the universal space has been expanded. Thus one may certainly expect that there must be a stage in the evolution of the Universe, when the effect of the dark energy would become stronger than gravitational attraction. From this stage on the universal expansion would exhibit acceleration. And this is exactly what astronomers found to be the case in 1998.

But then, as ordinary matter spread out and its gravitational pull diminished, the repulsive push of the cosmological constant (whose strength does not change as matter spreads out) would have gradually gained the upper hand, and *the era of decelerated spatial expansion would have given way to a new era of accelerated expansion.* (Greene 2004: 300, his italics)

If the nature of spacetime were relational, then spacetime could hardly possess such an intrinsic dynamic quality as dark energy. Energy is a fundamental property of material systems, and they have an existence of their own. So, we must concede that spacetime, possessing energy of its own, has also an existence of its own; or in other words, *it has a substantival nature.*

Spacetime demonstrates yet another property, which would hardly be conceivable for it to possess, if its nature were relational.

Since the birth of Einsteins general theory of relativity in 1916, it has been suggested that gravitational waves could exist. They are ripples in the curvature of spacetime that propagate as waves at the speed of light. One hundred years after Einstein hypothesized their existence, on February 11, 2016, the LIGO Scientific Collaboration and Virgo Collaboration teams (covering the international participation of scientists from several universities and research institutions) announced that they had made the first observation of gravitational waves. They originated from a pair of merging black holes being at a distance of 1.3 billion light years from the Earth, somewhere beyond the Large Magellanic Cloud in the southern hemisphere sky.

The observation of gravitational waves represents a clear argument in support of substantivalism. Relationalism could hardly account for the existence of such waves. Indeed, from a relationalist point of view, only material objects really exist, while space and time are specific relations among them. However, relations are relational *properties* of objects, and as being dependent on the specific configuration among objects, they have no existence of their own. But if so, relational properties cannot possess properties on their part, and in particular, a relational spacetime cannot initiate gravitational waves.

On the contrary, only if spacetime exists as an entity of its own and exhibits local curvatures responsible for the gravitational interaction, then collisions of massive cosmic objects like galaxies and black holes can certainly account for the appearance of gravitational waves. Thus the recent registration of gravitational waves is a convincing testimony for the substantival nature of spacetime.

8.4 Argument from a Consistent Interpretation of the Basic Equation in General Relativity

I have in mind the so called by A. Einstein field equation, or his well-known tensor equation of the general theory of relativity (the one hundred anniversary of the publication of which was celebrated four years ago):

$$R_{\alpha\beta} - \tfrac{1}{2} g_{\alpha\beta} R = \kappa T_{\alpha\beta}.$$

As is well known, the left side of this equation is usually called now Einstein's tensor, and it refers to the geometry of spacetime, but more ontologically speaking, to the entire set of spatial-temporal events. The tensor at the right side is the tensor of matter, known also by the name of energy-momentum tensor, and is taken to structurally represent the state and distribution of the different kinds of matter. However, Einstein himself had a problem concerning the construal of his field equation:

> But, it is similar to a building, one wing of which is made of fine marble (left part of the equation), but the other wing of which is built of low grade wood (right side of equation). The phenomenological representation of matter is, in fact, only a crude substitute for a representation which would correspond to all known properties of matter. (Einstein 1936: 370)

At that, there is another interpretative problem concerning the motion of material objects according to the general theory of relativity.

> The theory incorporates the effect of gravity by saying that the distribution of matter and energy in the universe warps and distorts spacetime, so that it is not flat. Objects in this spacetime try to move in straight

lines, but because spacetime is curved, their paths appear bent. They move as if affected by a gravitational field. (Hawking 2001: 35)

So, we are faced with a *curious situation*: material bodies warp spacetime, while at the same time spacetime curvatures determine the movement of material bodies.

The just outlined problems point to the need of a consistent interpretation of Einstein's basic equation of general relativity.

As it seems, there are two interpretative possibilities. The first one is to construe the equation as a standard equality of two different kinds of tensors, representing *independent kinds of entities* – Einstein's tensor and the matter tensor, which refer respectively to spacetime and to the distribution of matter and energy. At that, the tensor of matter is of a primary significance, since it is said that material bodies do cause the curvature of spacetime. In this case, however, the curious situation at hand could not be consistently elucidated. That is to say, this interpretation provides no arguable answer to the questions "Why, and how material objects warp space-time?"

The remaining alternative is to construe the equation as *expressing an identity*, and not merely a correlation of equality between its left and right sides. Thus both these sides ought to be taken as theoretical constructs that refer to one and the same entity. It is certainly represented by the "fine marble (left part of the equation)", or in other words, this initial entity is spacetime.[29]

There is another reason in favour of the identity interpretation, and it is of a logical character. As is well known, the covariant derivative of the tensor at the right part of the equation – the tensor of matter, or the energy-momentum tensor – must be zero. Applying covariant derivation includes the Christoffel symbols of the second kind (which are the affine connections of the four dimensional Riemannian spacetime). The Christoffel symbols, however, are functions of the metric tensor and its ordinary derivatives. Thus it comes out that in order to see whether the tensor at the right side of the equation is really a matter tensor, one has to know

---

[29] A tribute must be paid to Hermann Minkowski, who, as it seems, was the first to realize that the four-dimensionality of spacetime should not be accepted as a convenient descriptive language, but that the real physical world is four-dimensional. See in this connection V. Petkov (2013: 65-75).

beforehand the metric of the spacetime. This vicious circle could be overcome only by the identity interpretation, since within it spacetime and matter (or better say spacetime without and with material bodies) belong to one and the same initial, or fundamental essence.[30]

What is this fundamental essence?

It must be identified with spacetime, but not only with the geometry of spacetime, which turns out to be a main feature of this essence. This could certainly be neither "pure" spacetime, i.e. spacetime deprived of any material structures, nor "pure" matter without (or out of) spacetime, which even can hardly be conceived of. It could be provisionally named "prime-matter", or "primal matter", and so to remind us of the ancient Greek idea of a prim(aev)al essence giving birth to the variety of all visible and tangible natural objects, or of something like Anaximander's *apeiron*. When Einstein's tensor equals zero, then prime-matter is reduced to "empty" Riemannian spacetime; and when it is different from zero, then prime-matter presents itself as spacetime filled with material structures. Prime-matter is the fundamental essence that is looked for, since it unites spacetime as an entity described by a geometrical language with the material structures that are given birth within it.

The final conclusion in the end is that the identity interpretation of Einstein's equation of general relativity, being the only consistent one, certainly excludes the possibility for the relational nature of spacetime. It could be thought in no way as some set of relations among material objects whatsoever, because, just on the contrary, it is spacetime in its quality of prime-matter, which engenders material structures, and not vice-versa.

*

The conclusion in the end is that the arguments developed in sections 8.2 – 8.4 lend enough support to claim (C_8) stated at the beginning of this chapter and being its central claim, according to which in the relationalist-substantivalist debate preference has to be given to the substantival nature of spacetime.

---

[30] To my knowledge it was Anastassov (1973: 250) who raised for the first time the idea about such a fundamental essence.

9   TIME TRAVEL

9.1   Introductory Words

The subject about time travel displays both unfathomed theoretical depth, as well as unfaked human curiosity. This peculiarity seems to suppose successful decisions of all the problems the subject provokes. Needless to say, however, the problems concerning time travel are being still tackled by science fiction only, but not finally resolved by science proper neither theoretically, nor practically. So, the philosophical interest towards time travel is constantly growing.

The reason for this interest is not exhausted solely by the exotic character of the topic itself. As it has been noted, the answer about the possibility of time travel "depends on one's view concerning a wide range of other matters, and such views are themselves the subject of major philosophical controversy" (Varzi 2005: 325). The controversy spreads over diverse conceptions about the nature of time. Often, at that, misunderstandings occur, inspiring Paul Davies's revelation: "there has probably been more nonsense written by philosophers on the subject of time, from Plato onwards, than on any other topic" (1995: 252).

In order misunderstandings to be evaded, I shall take into account in the subsequent analyses not so much the intuitive notion of time, but some uncontroversial scientific results from the theory of relativity.

My aim in this chapter is to present some curious facts about time travel, to analyze different logical and ontological constraints that are presumed to prevent it and to outline three situations, for which time travel might be meaningfully contended. On the base of them I then put forward the *prima facie* "unexpected" claim

(C_9) Human conscious presence in the world is the genuine-and-natural time travel.

9.2   Curious Facts Concerning Time Travel

1) No officially registered case of a human being who has proved that she has visited us from the future or from the past

Let us suppose, as a joke, that somebody is insisting that she is visiting us from some future moment of time in comparison to our present. Then we may expect that she would be willing to inform her relatives about the final results of "today's" horse racing, and thus to make them rich people – something that will benefit her subsequently, as well. But either putative travelers in time are too moral to undertake such frauds, or all intendedly informed winners in horseracing games all over the world are suspiciously silent about the cause for their success.

2) Lack of empirical confirmation of time travel

What I mean here, is the lack of relevant confirmations of the kind that is needed for the establishment of a firm (and repeated) fact. Rare stories told by people to this effect, though published sometimes in newspapers and exotic books, do not go into scientific journals, and are thus not taken into account by the scientific community.

3) Lack of secure theoretical model for a "time machine"

The idea of time travel has still not been presented in the strict sense of a theoretical model that could work in principle on the basis of a definite physical conception of time, but is instead construed in broad "ideological" terms. This is so, because of the plurality of ontological concepts of time, each of which contains perplexities of its own. So, for all I know, the extant theoretical suggestions for time travels have not yet been proclaimed as implemented in a working technical device.

9.3 Ontological and Logical Constraints to Time Travel

Paradoxes of time travel.

a) *"Loop" paradoxes.* The paradox of the grandmother is a paradigmatic one of this sort. Let us assume that, provided I can travel in time, I go back into the past in the years when my grandmother was a young lady. Imagine further, that I have got some "good reason" to kill that woman (without knowing that she will become my grandmother), or simply inadvertently by driving a car. But if my grandmother was killed when she had not yet met and married my grandfather, then how possibly I could have been born, and then have grown up until the moment of my travel backwards in time?

b) *Changing the past.* If time travel were possible, then it would be also possible for me (at least in principle), by travelling into the past, to change some situation that has already passed away, but that has brought about some bad effect in my life. I didn't pay attention to the instructions of my guide when I went for an excursion to a high mountain for instance. I didn't take my new alpine shoes with me when climbing a steep peak; I slipped and fell, and broke my leg. And "now" I want to go back into my past, in order to correct my mistake. Although such an action seems to convey no logical contradiction, it appears to be ontologically impossible; because everything that has already happened, and is thus a constituent of *the frozen past,* cannot be changed (at least by my human will, fancy movies being left aside).[31]

The ontological aspect of the (a)-type and (b)-type paradoxes is usually illuminated by the assumed existence of so called *closed time-like curves* (CTCs). The existence of CTCs presupposes either an exotic topology of spacetime, or spinning black holes, or specific mass-energy distributions, all of which are not features of the (region of) spacetime, in which our Solar system is situated.[32]

---

[31] To this effect some authors admit that time travels are possible only into the future, and not into the past. But if this were the real state of affairs, then a time traveler would be doomed to spend the rest of her life in a world different, and eventually hostile to her acquired way of life, without any possibility to return to her "present" world. Hence such time travels could conceal unknown dangers for the curious adventurers.

[32] For a detailed account of CTCs see for instance (Mulder and Dieks 2016).

CTCs, really existent or not, could imply logical paradoxes as well. If one embarks on a space flight for example, and moves along a CTC, she could come back in the end at her starting point a minute before the rocket begins its flight, and could destroy it.

Similar ontological and logical embarrassments could appear concerning the possibility of backward travels in time with the purpose of changing one's past. The resulting paradoxes seem to reject namely *this* possibility, the attempt at changing past events, *that have already happened.* It does not ban time travels into the past in principle, when somebody could even be a participant in a historical situation, but does not change its course.[33] I'll go back to this option, no matter how curious it may seem, in the last section of the chapter.

A way out of (b)-type paradoxes is suggested within the *Many Worlds interpretation of quantum theory.* The gist of the interpretation is that *it successfully resolves the puzzle with the instantaneous reduction of the state function.* The well-known orthodox interpretation of quantum mechanics accepts all possible states that a quantum system could possess, as potential realities with different probabilities for realization. When observed, the system immediately "chooses" to be found in only *one* of its possible innumerous states. Instead, the Many Worlds conception postulates the *real* existence of *parallel universes,* each of which containing a possible outcome from the observation of a property of the system. Thus each universe is characterized by its unique state of affairs, comprised of a physical world together with the human beings whose conscious behavior (free will) has engendered the concrete universe.

The existence of parallel universes then could enable, at least in principle, such travelling back in time that is aimed at changing the past. I'll make use of Brian Greene's story to this effect, telling about a man who, lead by hatred, makes up his mind to kill his father several minutes before he has acquainted with his mother at a New Year party on December 31, 1965:

> When you travel to 11:50 p.m. on December 31, 1965, pull out your weapon, aim at your father, and pull the trigger, the gun works and you hit the intended target. But since this is not what happened in the universe from

---

[33] A nice explanation of this misunderstanding is provided by B. Dainton (2001: 112–3).

which you embarked on your time travel odyssey, your journey must not only have been through time, *it must have been also from one parallel universe to another.* The parallel universe in which you now find yourself is one in which your parents never did meet – a universe which the Many Worlds interpretation assures us is out there (since every possible universe consistent with the laws of quantum physics is out there). And so, in this approach, we face no logical paradox, because there are various versions of a given moment, each situated in a different parallel universe... In the universe of origination, your parents met on December 31, 1965, you were born, you grew up, you held a grudge against your father, you became fascinated with time travel, and you embarked on a journey to December 31, 1965. In the universe in which you arrive, your father is killed on December 31, 1965, before meeting your mother, by a gunman claiming to be his son from the future. A version of you is never born in this universe, but that's okay, since the you who pulled the trigger *does* have parents. It's just that they happen to live in a different parallel universe. Whether anyone in this universe believes your story or, instead, views you as delusional, I can't say. But what's clear is that in each universe – the one you left and the one you entered – we avoid self-contradictory circumstances. (Greene 2004: 457)

I agree with B. Greene that the Many Worlds interpretation affords changing the past, and even can resolve the above mentioned "loop" paradoxes. But it displays embarrassments of its own. One of them is of a purely existential character. If the son should go to prison after the murder of his potential father, against whom he has nursed a grudge, this act of murder is meaningful in the "original" universe, since only there it possesses a historical context. Killing innocent people in another universe is a sheer crime without any motivation. The second embarrassment concerns the high ontological price one pays when embracing the super realism of the Many Worlds interpretation. And the third concerns our original notion of freedom. At first glance the conception of the many universes seems to be a theoretical remedy against the difficulties of the unique block universe of the theory of relativity. But suppose that you are sitting at a table, and you are asked which of two refreshing drinks to order – tea or coffee? According to Paul Davies (1990: 141):

> [The Many Worlds] interpretation says that the universe immediately divides into two branches. In one of the branches you have tea, in the other coffee. This way you have everything!... Yet the victory seems a pyrrhic one. If you can't avoid making *all* possible choices, are you really free? The freedom seems overdone, destroyed by its own success. You want to choose tea *or* coffee, not tea *and* coffee.

c) *Impacts from the future.* Paradoxes of this type are not self-defeating loops like the (a)-type paradoxes, but allow for definite activities, inspired by information, coming from the future. A time traveler might become aware of circumstances not known within her proper present she has abandoned for a while, but which could affect her life on her arrival back into her present. I'll adduce here the curt example, suggested by B. Dainton (2001: 125). It considers the decision of a hesitating girl to settle her marriage.

> Mary is torn between two suitors. She can't decide whether to marry Tom or Jack. So she travels to the future and finds out that she is happily married to Tom. She then travels back, and marries Tom for this reason.

The paradoxical situation is based on the possible gain of information from the future, together with the *causal effect* this information can produce. The key words here are: "for this reason". Mary determines her own future as a married woman only in virtue of shedding a beam of light on moments of her future, without a live experience of the actual causes of her decision. What if her decision was due to a passing whim for instance? Anyhow, other options are possible: Mary might take either another decision (if only we believe in an open future), or take the same decision, but not "for this reason".

d) *The "discrepancy" paradox.* It appears whenever we assume that one embarks on a journey through time which takes far less time for its accomplishment than the span of time being traveled along. In Theodore Sider's words:

Before entering my time machine, I may say: "in two minutes I will gaze upon a dinosaur". This utterance appears paradoxical: how can the event of my gazing at the dinosaur be two minutes *after* my utterance (since, as I say, I "will" gaze at a dinosaur), and also two hundred million years *before* my utterance, back at the time of the dinosaurs? (Sider 2005: 329-330)

David Lewis paid special attention to this "discrepancy between time and time" (1986, 67). He suggested a way out of the paradox by discerning between "personal time" and "external time". The first is the time registered by the traveler in her time machine, while the second is grasped as time itself, as the amount of time that has been passed along, or covered, by the traveler into the past. D. Lewis' suggestion seems quite plausible, unless one gives herself account that the suggestion is not quite clear, having in mind the spacetime ontology of the theory of relativity. Within this ontology there is no "external time", analogous to the absolute time of Newton's theory, to be compared to "personal times". Each registered time is but a personal one.

One may contend, of course, that Lewis' "external time" is just the "personal time" for the Earth inhabitants from the time of the dinosaurs till now. If so, the paradox ceases to be a logical one, though still concealing an ontological conundrum (see the end of this section).

Non-paradoxical constraints
Does the arrow of time affect traveling in time?
As far as I am aware, the answer to this question has not been seriously analyzed. Probably there are two reasons for this.

The first one is the implicit belief in the symmetry of time, in so far as the fundamental physical laws are invariant in relation to the change of the time variable t with $-t$. The idea of the homogeneity of time stays in support to this belief. In addition to that, if the flow of time is mind-dependent, while spacetime – in accordance with the theory of relativity – is four-dimensional with time being one of its dimensions, then whatever "direction" of time is hardly imaginable.

The second reason is the yet non-elucidated answer to the question "What is the arrow of time?" There are different pretenders

to be *the* arrow of time, and they are even not all equally directed
– e.g. the thermodynamic arrow of time, based on the increase
of entropy (and unidirectional with the cosmological one), and the
"historical", pointing to the permanent emergence of highly or-
ganized (biological and technical) systems, thus requiring a local
decrease of entropy.

It is often declared that the arrow of time is marked by the
course of change of the so called irreversible processes. But the
fundamental problem arises whether these processes determine the
arrow of time, or they are possible, because there *is* an arrow of
time. It seems that the second option relies on deeper arguments
than the first, among which are the simple, but convincing thought
experiment suggested by D.H. Mellor (1998, 120–121). I have envisaged a short presentation of the ontological status of the arrow
of time, as well as a part of Mellor's reasoning in *Appendix B*.

What I can say as an answer right now is the following. If there
is an arrow of time itself – and there are cogent arguments that the
universe is "lopsided" [34] – then it may certainly affect time travel.
Although common sense has proved to be not a good advisor in
theoretical research, I find the contention that travelling against
the arrow of time is, if not entirely forbidden, at least subject to
definite limitations, to be trustworthy. It might be the case that it
is namely due to the arrow of time that (a)-type loop paradoxes,
as well as actions intended to change settled events from the past,
are hardly possible to occur in our world.

Where to go?

According to our contemporary established knowledge traveling
in time is related to traveling in space, too. This follows from the
spacetime ontology of general relativity, in which space and time
are indivisibly intertwined in a *four-dimensional spacetime*. This
implies that a "movement" from one four-dimensional event within
spacetime to another one, would represent a transfer through time,
as well. So, if somebody wants to visit her future or her past at
an exactly chosen moment, she has to take into account also her
space position at the final point of the travel. For it would be a
disappointment, if one wants to travel back in time, say 90 years
ago, in order to become witness of her grandfather's success in the

---

[34] Such arguments are examined by Paul Davies, (1995: 208–218).

elections for a President of The United States, and to find herself to be in the same remote year in London, instead of in Washington.

A suspicion may arise, however, that *every event in spacetime is equally well accessible from a previously chosen one.* At least, we have no reliable proof in favour of this claim. The twin (known also as the clocks) paradox, that I shall comment below, assures us that some types of travel in spacetime are possible, and that one can – at least in principle – visit his brother twin in his future. But the claim that it probably would not be possible for one to travel from her spacetime position to another spacetime destination that she has arbitrarily chosen to visit, represents a specific ontological constraint for time travelers.

This exactly was the point in the end of my comment to the (d)-paradox concerning the possibility of gazing at living ancient dinosaurs, when I said that even if we remove the paradoxical element, there still remains an ontological conundrum. The conundrum if such positions from the remote past are ever accessible to us – either principally, or technologically.

9.4   My Thesis

My thesis is that there are three possibilities a time-travel to be realized. The first two of them are possibilities only in principle. The third is a possibility that has been permanently realized as the natural way of being in the world for humans – the conscious grasping of the surrounding world as a world evolving through time. I call this *a genuine-and-natural travel in time.*

In other words, the second part of my thesis coincides with the content of claim (C_9) in the end of section 9.1.

The first possibility is expressed by the already mentioned *twin paradox.* It is worth noticing right now, that the naming of this well-known relativistic effect a "paradox" is an obsolete one, since the effect is not paradoxical in itself, as some people once accepted. But this name has strengthen its use to such an extent, that any change of it may lead to misunderstandings. I'll make a short presentation of the twin paradox for two reasons. First, to show why it offers a time-travel, and second, to use it as an argument in favour of the static conception of time (represented by B-theories of time) instead of the dynamic one (represented by A-theories of

112

time).

Let us suppose that the one of two identical twins, symbolized by A, remains on Earth, while the other – symbolized by B – undertakes a space voyage with a rocket ship flying very fast. He reaches a goal point G (e.g. some planet around a distant star), and returns to Earth to see his brother twin again. Denoting the spacetime point of departure with D, and the spacetime point of the meeting of the twins with M, let us further suppose that the elapsed time for twin A, who remained on Earth, is $\Delta t_A = 10$ years. It is well known then, that the respective time interval (between the same events D and M) for twin B will be $\Delta t_B < \Delta t_A$. If the speed of B's space ship is great enough,[35] it could be the case, that when twin B returns to Earth, the time that has passed for him is twice shorter than his brother's, i.e. $\Delta t_B = 5$ years – see Fig.1.

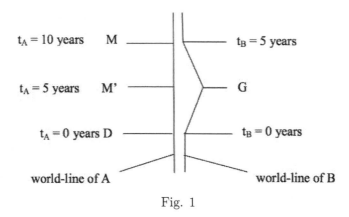

$t_A = 10$ years   M _____ _____ $t_B = 5$ years

$t_A = 5$ years   M' _____ _____ G

$t_A = 0$ years D _____ _____ $t_B = 0$ years

world-line of A   world-line of B

Fig. 1

Thus, when the twins meet in M, the one who remained on Earth, A, will be 5 years older than his brother twin B. But this means that B meets his brother in a future moment of his life. While on Earth 10 years have passed away since B's departure, B has experienced only 5 years. He arrives back to see his planet being 5 years ahead from his 5 years that he, and his space ship, have really gone through. *His adventure is a travel in time.* The faster his space ship could fly, the further into the future he could

[35] It could be easily calculated (by using the Lorentz transformations) that the speed of the ship in this case must be about 261 thousand km/s.

visit the world he once left for his cosmic trip.

One may say that such an experiment has not yet been carried out. This is true of course, and the reason is trivial: the lack of appropriate technical possibilities for the realization of the experiment. The twin paradox, however, as a direct consequence from the special theory of relativity, has been observed many times as the effect of prolongation of the life time of fast moving elementary particles.[36]

Now let us see whether the dynamic view of time can explain the twin paradox. As we know, according to this view the flow of time is real, and the world events possess reality only when they are elements of the present. Past events do not already exist, and future events do not yet exist. Thus the physical presence of the twins is realized by their three-dimensional bodies changing in time. But if so, 5 years after his departure twin B will exist in the event M, and will not be able to meet his brother, since for the *same* period of time twin A will exist at M' – in the middle of his history between the event of the departure D and the event of the meeting M. (Let me remind that 10 years are needed for twin A to meet his brother.) The dynamic view fails to explain the twin paradox.

On the contrary, the static conception of time provides a sound explanation. According to it, past, present, and future events possess one and the same ontological status, they are equally real. Twins A and B are existing in the world with the whole of their history, and particularly by their world lines between the events D and M. But if their four-dimensional bodies are actually present between these two events, they will surely meet at the event of B's arrival on Earth. The result of the twin paradox – B's seeing the future of his world he once left – is easily explained by the fact that the (four-dimensional) world line of B is twice shorter than the world line of A.[37] Since the personal time of the twins is measured

---

[36] "Amazingly, particle physicists have to take this time dilation into account when they are dealing with particles that decay. In the lab, muon particles typically decay in 2.2 microseconds. But fast moving muons, such as those created when cosmic rays strike the upper atmosphere, take 10 times longer to disintegrate." https://cosmosmagazine.com/physics/five-ways-travel-through-time

[37] Looking at the drawing of Fig.1 imposes just the opposite impression: the world line of twin A is shorter than that of twin B. The reason for this misrepresentation is the fact that the twins' world lines are represented on the

along their respective world lines (personal histories), A's time is twice longer than B's time between the events D and M. Thus according to the static conception of time, being in harmony with the theory of relativity, (the passage of time is mind-dependent and) there are as much personal times, as is the number of observers to be found in relative motion among each other.

This is just an additional argument to those that were adduced already in section 2.2 in support of the view about the actual existence of the four-dimensional spacetime.

The second possibility for time-travels is prompted by the features of physical spacetime, according to the general theory of relativity. It is mathematically modeled by a four-dimensional Riemannian geometrical space (comprised of three space and one time dimensions). Traveling in spacetime means then accomplishing a movement from one spacetime physical event (represented by one point of the Riemannian space) to another spacetime event (to another point of this space). But such movements cannot be arbitrarily accomplished, because they ought to satisfy some rules, and probably the constraints outlined in section 9.3.

Thus it seems that the class of possible time-travels is reduced to movements within spacetime, represented by translations – and may be not by closed curves – that are free from paradoxical and other ontological limitations. I say "within" spacetime, since a translation carried out "over" spacetime is hardly possible. Such a travel would require additional space and time-like dimensions to enable the intended journey as "sliding over" the four-dimensional manifold. For all we know, such dimensions, even if we hypothetically think that they are "out there", are not at our disposal.

But there is another possibility of traveling in time. It is based on the well-known idea of using hypothetical *worm-holes* in the texture of space-time. Thus time-travel would be possible not *over* space-time, but *through* holes *within* it. For now, candidates for gates of spacetime worm-holes are the *black holes*. According to Carl Sagan's optimistic opinion:

> An object that plunges down a rotating black hole may

Euclidian surface of the sheet of paper, while in reality these lines lie within a pseudo-Euclidian space. Its inhomogeneous metrics contributes to the opposite result. A clear explanation of it could be found for example in (Penrose 1989: 255-256). See also (Petkov 2005: 142-146).

> re-emerge elsewhere and elsewhen – in another place
> and another time. Black holes may be apertures to
> distant galaxies and to remote epochs. They may be
> shortcuts through space and time. (Sagan 1975: 264)

If this is true, namely that we can rely on black holes to transfer us to remote epochs, we have to concede that gazing at dinosaurs two hundred million years from "now" is not an impossible adventure.

Unfortunately, this possibility remains only as a speculative project. As it is known, this idea is committed to serious obstacles. "Plunging down" a black hole for instance is not safe, since the huge gravitational gradient would tear apart the cosmic traveler together with her flying device.

The same idea may involve a suitable "engenering" of spacetime, so that a worm-hole (a tunnel through spacetime) to be constructed, which could lead from one's present to a past or a future place in spacetime, no matter how remote those places could be compared to the one's starting point. Worm-holes provide hypothetically direct connections between places in spacetime being so far away from each other, that an ordinary journey between them would last thousands of years with the speed of light. However, the construction of a worm-hole through spacetime conceals not only putative practical difficulties, but meets purely conceptual embarrassments as well. They are related with providing stability of the worm-hole construction, which presupposes the keeping of negative energy density for a negative curvature of the chosen spacetime region, which is hardly possible on a quantum level.[38]

The conclusion so far allows for a specific class of time-travels, representing (relatively small) positional shifts in spacetime that comply with the already discussed ontological constraints. An evidence for this hypothesis may be the rarely published stories of people pretending to have really experienced time travels, if we take them seriously, of course. If not, we may accept that such time travels are possible only in principle. Nobody has proved, indeed, that she has constructed a working time-machine.

A further comment is needed, however, concerning the hypothetical time-travels. Let us suppose for example, that we read a

---

[38] A detailed account of these problems can be found for example in (Hawking 2001: ch. 5) and (Hawking and Mlodinow 2005: ch.10.).

newspaper story about a curious discovery of a palaeontological expedition: a human shoe-print around the big petrified foot-prints of an ancient dinosaur, dating from one and the same epoch. Let us suppose further that, believing the story, we do not believe that humans resided the Earth together with dinosaurs. As it seems, the only conclusion left then is to concede that a clever man from the future has managed to construct a time-machine, and has successfully achieved a long distance time trip into the past.

But this may not be the only explanation. Besides, as we already know, backward time-travels meet the constraint of not changing the past. This constraint is a very delicate one, because even slight changes of details that constitute the past, can eventually lead to sizable changes in the future. Then, what other explanation we may rely on?

This is an explanation which attracts *no actual time travel*. If the static conception of time is to be preferred instead of the dynamic one (since it better complies with the spacetime ontology of the theory of relativity), then a possibility, although strangely looking, may be envisaged. The possibility that for some, yet unknown, reason, or simply occasionally, the otherwise integral history of an object can be separated into temporal parts, situated within different places of spacetime. Thus a temporal part of the four-dimensional body channel of an individual may be laid in another region of spacetime. In such a way the individual could take part in forming the past, without changing it. In this sense Barry Dainton admits the activity of a man from our present who takes part in the building activities of the Egyptian pyramids.

You may have been born in 1975, but unbeknownst to you and your parents this was not your first appearance in the world's affairs: you first entered history as a thirty year old, assisting with the building of the pyramids several thousand years previously. In short, everything that you will ever do as a time traveller is *built into the past* before your first journey. Prior to your departure you do not remember being in Egypt all those years ago, but this is because the time you spend there lies in your (personal) future. Of course, if you left any traces of your visit – perhaps you carved your initials on a sarcophagus – these may well be discovered prior to your departure. It is one thing to *affect* the past – to contribute to what occurred at the times in question – quite another to *change* it. You certainly affected the past – your initials are a testament to that, and there are Egyptian slaves who were glad of your help – but you did not change it. The building of the pyramids only occurred once, and you were there at the time (Dainton 2001: 113, his italics).

B. Dainton does not speak about temporal parts, but only such a "division" of a personal human history could explain the suggested example of one's existence into the past without changing it. I called such a possibility "strange" , but as it seems, it can be qualified as impossible, in so far as such a division of the temporal parts of an entity *keeping an identity to itself* would drastically disturb the spacetime region of its residence; and that appears to be a process staying out of the control of the known physical laws.

In the end, I come to *the third possibility of traveling in time*, which I find to be the natural human existence in the world. This is the real humanlike way of life, based on the perception of the surrounding world as a reality, given to human sensitive faculty, and turned to be temporalized by it. No matter how "Kantian" this may seem, but we already know (as a corollary of the static conception) that the passage of time is mind-dependent.

Human beings *are* travelers in time. They experience time through perceiving changes in events and among events, as well as through the sense of duration. *Time-travel is thus expressed in the human awareness of change and duration*, despite that the four-dimensional world neither changes, nor has any duration along an additional time dimension.

I call this a genuine-and-natural travel in time.

Positively interpreted, time-travel is but the conscious grasp of the world, when human consciousness "sheds light" upon the consecutive events along the unique world-tube, encompassed by a man's living body (i.e. along the whole man's history). Here we come to the shortly expressed content of claim (C_9) in the end of section 9.1, which stays in full harmony with the elaborated BA-theory of time proposed in section 4.4.

Metaphysically interpreted, the genuine-and-natural travel in time is the permanent revealing of Being by the unique human mode of being. It is the temporal stretch of human existence. And it has its human limits: we can remember the past, can be active in the present, and are not certain for the future.[39]

In other words, the genuine-and natural time travel is the unique, purely human way of one being aware of the world – the way of the world as being unveiled to human consciousness as a non-ceasing sequence of life events. Man has no divine power to present for himself the entire world at once, even not his entire life-span. Otherwise, man would lose his essence – the feeling for freedom.

---

[39] "It is not for you to know times or seasons which Father has put in His own authority." The Acts 1:7.

10 Conclusion

The first sentence from the *Introduction* states that "This book is comprised of interconnected philosophical analyses of conceptions of space, time, and spacetime." I cherish the hope that I have succeeded in fulfilling the pretension of this declaration. I made my attempt to set out and to critically analyze different conceptions of space, time, and spacetime. I have also suggested nine claims distributed in each one of the chapters of the book from the second to the ninth one, and I have tried to provide arguments for these claims.

Maybe all this could have been done in a better way.

To my mind, this being so, or not, is not the most important fact about the content of this work. What is more important, at least for me, is what I have mentioned in the already quoted first sentence that the presented analyses are *interconnected*. The intended meaning of this attribute here is that the proposed claims in the different chapters are in harmony with each other, and that *the respective argumentations are "complementary" among themselves*. This intention of mine was not declared in advance because of sustaining a correct attitude to the reader. If I am right, the reader could probably feel this intention when reaching the end of the whole story told in this book. This way or not, each chapter can be read separately from the others, skipping the reference notes being often made among their respective subject matters.

Now I'll say a few words about what I mean when saying that the arguments I have tried to expose in defense of the claims raised in the different chapters are "complementary".

I mean by this only one thing – that the argumentations from the different chapters have both overlapping and not overlapping parts, but leading together to outlining a consistent conception of spacetime and the way it is represented in our direct experience.

The physical existence of spacetime is conjectured not only because of the high degree of corroboration of the theory of relativity, but because the traditional common view of space and time (presented in section 2.1) has proved to be theoretically inadequate, and because it also exhibits different paradoxes (section 2.3), in spite of its intuitive clarity. I agree in this connection with the shared confession of some contemporary authors that the world is different from the way it is depicted by our direct sense representations, being susceptible though to our knowledge based on our theoretical efforts (section 2.2). Let me repeat Brian Greene's conviction (2011: 5) that

> If there was any doubt at the turn of the twentieth century, by the turn of the twenty-first, it was a foregone conclusion: when it comes to revealing the true nature of reality, common experience is deceptive.

Common experience has turned out to be deceptive concerning the flow of time. The latter may be determined then to be mind-dependent, i.e. to be a subjective phenomenon of the human way of perceiving the world, but not to be an objective process within physical reality. How the flow of time is endowed with empirical reality, if time does not really flow (being a constituent of spacetime) was shown in chapter 6. This was also the conceptual framework for the proposal of the elaborated BA-theory of time in chapter 4. And it stays in harmony with the basic claim of chapter 9 which states that "human conscious presence in the world is the genuine-and-natural time travel".

The elaborated BA-theory of time reveals an intimate connection between time and consciousness, and we ought to pay attention to it. Otherwise we shall stay in astonishment about our existence as conscious beings. Or to repeat the confession made by Paul Davies (1995: 278):

> Elucidating the mysterious [time] flux would, more than anything else, help unravel the deepest of all scientific enigmas – the nature of the human self. Until we have a firm understanding of the flow of time, or incontrovertible evidence that it is indeed an illusion, then we

will not know who we are, or what part we are playing in the great cosmic drama.

The elaborated BA-theory of time elucidates the connection between time and consciousness by taking seriously Weyl's idea about consciousness to be crawling upward along the world-lines (or better say along the world-tubes) of our bodies. The dispositional property of time for A-properties enables this, and I take this dispositional property to be the temporal asymmetry, which is manifested by the cosmological, the thermodynamic, and the psychological arrows of time (section 4.4). Thus the relativistic picture of the world is reconciled with our clear experience of time flow.

122

A ZENO'S PARADOXES AND THE FAILURE OF THEIR ALLEGED SOLUTIONS BASED ON THE COMMON VIEW OF SPACE AND TIME

This *Appendix* appears with the aim to fulfil my promise at the end of section 2.3 the most popular out of the Zeno's paradoxes to be analyzed together with the failure of their no less popular solutions, based on the ideology of the traditional common view of space and time.

Zeno's paradoxes are permanently attracting the philosophers' interest, resulting in hundreds of research works, as well as of popular essays in textbooks and websites. They emerge in their quality of *aporiae* that is to say of impasses, of problem situations without an exit, what is the original meaning of the Greek word *"aporia"*.

There is no unanimous opinion why Zeno formulated his paradoxes of motion. According to the standard and, as it seems, most popular view, he wanted to reject the belief that motion is a genuine process of spatial change through time, since its logical analyses lead to contradictions.

There are two camps of thinkers. The shared opinion within the first camp is that Zeno's paradoxes have already obtained their solutions by using mathematical means or dialectical reasoning. Thinkers within the other camp reject this optimistic opinion. I'll try to show that they have strong arguments to do so.

Dichotomy

This paradox of Zeno has two versions. According to the first one a runner, starting her quick movement from point A, can never reach a final goal point B. The reason for this conviction is that the runner must firstly reach the middle of the way between A and B, then the middle point of the remaining half of the way, then the middle point of the remaining quarter of the distance to point B, and so on, and so forth. Since space is infinitely divisible, the runner has to pass through infinite number of points in a finite interval of time; and in so far as this is impossible, she will never reach the end point B.

The second version of "Dichotomy" states that the runner can never be set in motion, because before reaching the middle point between A and B, she must have passed through the middle point of the first half of the intended distance, but before that she must have reached the middle point of the first quarter of the distance, and so on. Thus there is no possibility for the runner to start her running process, which means that a movement from A to B is impossible.

Authors like Nicholas Fearn, for instance, see no difficulty in resolving the first version of "Dichotomy". In the times of Zeno, he contends, people had the false impression that a distance, composed of infinite parts, though diminishing in size, must be infinitely long. But it is known now that the sum S

$$S = \frac{1}{2} + \frac{1}{4} + \cdots + \frac{1}{2^n} + \cdots$$

of the dichotomized segments of any distance included between two different points A and B is finite, and equals 1. Thus our runner covers a finite distance in a finite interval of time, and this is all.[40]

The first version of "Dichotomy" cannot be resolved, however, in the suggested way. What Zeno seems to have adduced as an aporetical argument is not the claim about the infinite magnitude of the sum S, notwithstanding whether he believed in that, or not. His argument is that the runner is not able to actually pass through an infinite number of spatial points in a finite interval of time. And exactly this impossibility implies the impossibility of motion, and hence, its nonreality.

The same reasoning is valid for the second version of "Dichotomy".

As it seems, the paradox could not be obviated by leaving its ontological background intact. Its central assumption is that space

---

[40] See the third essay "Zeno and the Tortoise" in (Fearn 2001).

is a dense set of points, i.e. it is a continuum. A negation of this assumption is the claim that space is a discrete set of elements, or in other words, that its deep structure is a grain structure, that it is comprised of specific and further indivisible spatial atoms. To this effect there are authors who attract the ontology of quantum mechanics. But this step can hardly be of any help for seeking a plausible solution, since the quantum world exhibits complexities of its own. For example, we have no evidence, and we can have no evidence in principle, how a free quantum particle "moves" from point A to point B, and for all we know, it could realize its "motion" in many different ways, each bearing its own probability for realization.

The ancient Aristotelian solution, making difference between actual and potential infinity, has certainly a heuristical merit (to be elaborated further by H. Bergson, as we shall see below), but offers no clear solution, too. This is the reason for Hegel to agree with Bayle's judgment that Aristotle's answer to "Dichotomy" is, uttered in French, "pitoyable".[41]

Achilles and the Tortoise

Let us imagine now that our hero is the legendary Achilles, who starts his quick run in a race with a slowly moving tortoise to be found 10 meters ahead of him. The curious conclusion in this paradox of Zeno is that the fleet-footed Achilles will never be able to overtake the tortoise in the running race – a fact that obviously contradicts our everyday experience. And it is just through this curious conclusion that the illusionary phenomenon of motion was meant to be proved once again. How this conclusion is made?

If we accept that our hero runs with a speed $v = 1$ m/s (one meter per second), and the tortoise moves ahead with a speed $u = 0.01$ m/s (one centimeter per second), after the first second from the beginning of the race Achilles is to be found one meter after the starting point, and 9.01 m behind the tortoise. After two seconds he shall be 8.02 m behind the tortoise, then 7.03 m behind it, etc. Although the distance between the two competitors is constantly diminishing, Achilles shall always be *behind* the tortoise, because during each interval of time in which he manages to reach the point where the tortoise was found in front of him, the slow animal will

---

[41]That is to say, piteous, deplorable (Hegel 1892: 269).

manage to pass a new distance ahead of him. Thus Achilles will never be able to catch up with the tortoise.

It is worth noticing that this paradox could be transformed into the first one, i.e. into "Dichotomy". If our coordinate system is not attached to the earth, but to the moving tortoise, then Achilles ought to cover the distance between his starting point and the immovable tortoise, a distance between two fixed points, A and B. This transformation is possible, because of the equivalent character of the two coordinate systems attached to two inertial frames of reference. This dodge provides no solution to "Achilles and the tortoise", however, unless we possessed a plausible solution to "Dichotomy", and this is not the case.

A "strides solution" is often put to the fore. In our case this suggestion for a solution takes into account that Achilles' stride per second is hundred times longer than that of the tortoise. So, ten seconds after the beginning of the race, Achilles shall be 10 m after his starting point, while the tortoise – 10.1 m after it. After one more second the slow animal shall be 10.11 m after Achilles' starting point, but Achilles himself – 11 m after it, which would mean that he has overtaken his competitor, and is already 0.89 m ahead of her. This commonsensical "solution", however, walks past the gist of the paradox, that in order to cover the 11 centimeters distance to the tortoise moving ahead of him, Achilles must accomplish infinite acts of crossing over the always remaining spatial intervals separating (the mass center of) his body from that of the moving tortoise for a finite interval of time, less than a second.

It could be also contended that the considered paradox has a mathematical solution, resembling the analogous "solution" to "Dichotomy". Let the initial distance between Achilles and the tortoise is indicated by d, the speed of the running Achilles by v, and that of the tortoise by u. The time needed for the swift-footed hero to reach the first position of the tortoise is $t_1 = d/v$. The time needed for him to reach the second position of the animal, which in the meantime has moved a distance ut_1, is $t_2 = ut_1/v$, the next third time for reaching the third position of the tortoise is $t_3 = ut_2/v = t_1 u^2/v^2$, and so on, and so forth. Thus the time needed for Achilles to reach the n-th position of the tortoise is $t_n = (u/v)^{n-1}t_1$. The expression for the sum of the infinite row of time intervals for reaching the ever shifting ahead tortoise's positions is

$$T = \sum_{n=1}^{\infty} t_n = \sum_{n=1}^{\infty} \left(\frac{u}{v}\right)^{n-1} t_1.$$

This infinite row is a geometrical progression with a multiplier $u/v < 1$, and it is easily obtained that

$$T = \frac{d}{v - u}.$$

This result means that our running hero can come up with his slow competitor in a finite interval of time that is as close to t_1, as v is greater than u. Evidently the result completely agrees with everyday experience, but still can hardly be taken to be a *solution* of the paradox under consideration. And this is so, because Zeno's intention was not to deny that Achilles is able to catch up with the tortoise in a finite period of time, but that just within this finite period of time he can never actualize an infinite number of crossings of the spatial segments that separate him from the moving tortoise, no matter how a slow "runner" she is.

The Arrow

Probably, by this paradox Zeno wanted to show the contradictory nature of motion, not only when it is thought to be a process of transition through continuous space during the time's flow of a finite interval of time, but also when it is accepted to be a consecutive change of spatial places, which a moving body occupies in different fixed moments of time. By contrast with the former two cases, "The Arrow" is a paradox accepting motion to be realized not by virtue of the hypothesis about continuous time, but on the basis of the assumption that time is a sequence of discrete moments.[42]

Let us imagine the flight of a swift arrow, and let us also accept that time is a sequence of constantly changing indivisible moments, a permanent sequence of "nows" (of present moments). Within an arbitrary moment "now", the arrow has to be immovable, since

---

[42]Another argument of Zeno, known as *Stadium*, also leads to a paradox, if space and time are admitted to have a discrete structure, i.e., if they are constituted by "atoms" of space and of time that are not further divisible into smaller spatial or time intervals.

if it were in motion, the fixed moment "now" should be divisible into parts, each corresponding to the places in space, occupied by the arrow. But this conclusion contradicts our premise that the moment "now" is further indivisible, being the smallest discrete interval of time. So, the time of the flight of the arrow is comprised just by such "nows", it is a sequence of discrete time intervals, and within every such "atom" of time the arrow occupies a fixed spatial volume, which is the place of the arrow corresponding to each specific "now". But it follows from here that the arrow is not flying at all, because *it is at rest within each "atom" of time*, and a sequence of states of rest can never produce a state of motion.

In order an exit from this *aporia* to be found, that saves motion as a real phenomenon, some philosophers seek a refuge in dialectics. A dialectical solution to "The Arrow" is expected to be even universal to all paradoxes of motion as well, since this solution turns the paradoxical conclusions, traditionally taken to be a weak point in the philosophical defense of the reality of motion, into an argument in its favour. This transformation is based on evaluative change of the logical contradiction, from a negative into a positive feature explicated by the phenomenon of motion. And it was just "The Arrow" paradox that has given rise to the *paradigmatic dialectical solution*, or PDS for short, prompted by dialectical reasoning:

(PDS) At every instant of time the flying arrow *is* found, *and is not* found at a definite place.

The dialectical view accepts the truth of the phenomenon of motion together with its contradictory character. And if motion has to be treated in this way, it should be also claimed that it is something more than its standard trajectory presentation through a mathematical function of the spatial position of a moving body defined on the time variable. This is so, because the standard mathematical presentation of motion, being formal and thus a non-contradictory one, presupposes that a moving body has always a strict position in space corresponding to every instant from the duration of the process of motion. In this way, the standard mathematical presentation describes only *the effect of motion, but is not a presentation of its nature*. According to the dialectical treatment motion is *contradictory in itself*.

In order to get movement into the picture, according to dialectic, we must recognize both that the body is at that place and that, in the same instant, it is also ceasing to be so. For our description needs to capture the fact not only that the body is where it is, but also that it is moving – hence in a process of change and becoming. For this contradiction is essential. As Hegel (...) says, 'something moves not because at one moment it is here and at another there, but because at one and the same moment it is here and not here.' (Sayers 1991, 87)

So, for a genuine (Hegelian and Marxist) dialectician motion (and more generally every change) is, in Hegel's words, an "existent contradiction" , and this is the nature of motion, which in no way could be captured by pure mathematical or formal logical presentations. But can the dialectical approach, resulting in its paradigmatic claim that at every instant the flying arrow occupies and does not occupy a definite volume of space, be accepted as a resolution to Zeno's paradoxes?

I pose this question seriously, so I don't expect the probably correct, but trivial answer that dialecticians would reply with "yes," and non-dialecticians – with "no." What a philosopher cherishes above all in accepting a claim as a solution to a paradox is that claim to be grounded on a sound argumentation. This means that if behind the PDS stands a consistent argumentation produced in a proper dialectical pattern, then one must accept PDS as (at least a feasible) solution to Zeno's paradoxes, even if she is not an adherent to dialectics. But is this the case with PDS?

My answer is "no." Although PDS rests on a dialectical formulation, it still lacks an appropriate dialectical argumentation. The notion of contradiction is central for dialectics. It results in the unity and the struggle of opposites. Moreover, the gist of the dialectical approach is the explanation of the dynamical phenomena in nature and the development of social processes through solutions of the contradictions leading to some new state of affairs. The latter is always an outcome from the struggle of the former opposites, and is expressed by a claim about synthesis of a thesis and an anti-thesis. But this well elaborated dialectical scheme is hardly applicable to the "Arrow paradox," i.e. to the paradox of mechanical motion. Within the phenomenon of mechanical motion the combating opposites are not clearly differentiated. The involvement of the abstract concepts of continuity and discontinuity for this purpose is still insufficient for a clear picture of opposites in a struggle, and the realization of a synthesis as a solution to the alleged contradiction is still more unclear.

PDS remains a very general statement, dependent on how the paradigmatic dialectical formula "A and non-A" is being interpreted, while there is no unanimously accepted interpretation among philosophers and logicians. Thus PDS can pretend for the most to be some conceptual framework for understanding the "Arrow paradox," but not a proper solution to it.

In his *Creative Evolution*, Henri Bergson declares to have surmounted Zeno's paradoxes of motion.

> Take the flying arrow. At every moment, says Zeno, it is motionless... Yes, if we suppose that the arrow can ever be in a point of its course. Yes again, if the arrow, which is moving, ever coincides with a position, which is motionless. *But the arrow never is in any point of its course.* The most we can say is that it might be there, in this sense, that it passes there and might stop there. It is true that if it did stop there, it would be at rest there, and at this point it is no longer movement that we should have to do with. The truth is that if the arrow leaves the point A to fall down at the point B, its movement AB is as simple, as indecomposable, in so far as it is movement, as the tension of the bow that shoots it... Suppose an elastic stretched from A to B, could you divide its extension? The course of the arrow is this very extension; it is equally simple and equally undivided. It is a single and unique bound. You fix a point C in the interval passed, and say that at a certain moment the arrow was in C. If it had been there, it would have been stopped there, and you would no longer have had a flight from A to B, but two flights, one from A to C and the other from C to B, with an interval of rest. A single movement is entirely, by the hypothesis, a movement between two stops; if there are intermediate stops, it is no longer a single movement. (Bergson 1911: 308-309, my italics)

The key point in this quotation is the bold claim that "the

arrow never is in any point of its course." If this claim was not taken seriously, then the other metaphorical contentions of Henri Bergson to the effect that the course of the arrow is an "extension" resembling that of stretched elastic from point A to point B, and that the motion of the arrow represents a simple and indivisible act, would sound no more than curious assertions. Probably Bergson has learned well the Aristotle's lesson that in considering Zeno's paradoxes one must give up operating with actual infinity and thus must not direct her attention at the trajectory of a body that has already ceased its motion, since the line of the trajectory is a dense and actually infinite set of spatial points. The phenomenon of motion should not be explained through its result, when a moving body has already stopped to move, but should be construed as an "extension," as an indivisible bound through space. So, the claim that an arrow starting from point A and ending its flight at point B has passed through point C as well, has no proper meaning, unless the arrow has stopped in C, is motionless in C, and then has resumed its flight from C to B. Otherwise we cannot meaningfully assert for a body in motion that it is in point C at a definite moment of time.

Bergson pretends also that his conception about the phenomenon of motion provides a simple solution to "Achilles and the tortoise" paradox.

> When Achilles pursues the tortoise, each of his steps must be treated as indivisible, and so must each step of the tortoise. After a certain number of steps, Achilles will have overtaken the tortoise. There is nothing more simple. (Ibid: 311)

Can we accept Bergson's exhortation that "there is nothing more simple"? I think that the answer is "no," at least for two reasons. His suggested solution is but the already considered "strides solution," and we saw that it does not meet the conceptual challenge of the paradox. At that, his "simple" solution is not quite consistent with his own view of the nature of motion. Indeed, if Achilles has undertaken a swift run, then, as Bergson clearly insists, his body should be involved in an indivisible act of motion. But why then Achilles' steps should be considered separately from one another, as if the fleet-footed hero stops and resumes his dash with every step of him?

Let us turn back to the central idea of Bergson's conception of motion. It is expressed by the claim that a flying arrow is never found in any point of its course at any instant of the duration of its flight.

What does this claim mean, and what is its explanatory import for the solution of "The arrow" paradox?

At first glance, Bergson's central claim resembles the dialectical solution expressed by the PDS. For in both attempts at solving the paradox it is asserted that at every instant the arrow does not occupy a definite place in space. We have come to the conclusion that PDS is not a proper solution to "The arrow" paradox, but a general conceptual framework for its construal. The case with Bergson's central claim is even worse, since Bergson does not even have the potential of the dialectical scheme at his disposal.

As for the explanatory import of Bergson's claim one may say that in its quality of a general assumption it could have the only pretension "to save the phenomenon" of motion, and not to explain its possibility and hence its reality. So, the proposed solution by Bergson to Zeno's paradoxes can attract, on its part, the old Bayle's qualification: "pitoyable".

The failure of the considered solutions to the most popular of Zeno's paradoxes is due to the fact that they are incorporated into the common view of space and time, which has a phenomenological backing. According to this classical view space and time have autonomous existence in separation from each other. As we know this common view of space and time was superseded by the relativistic picture based on the concept of spacetime. Time is not an entity, flowing or not, which is separate from space, but it is a constituent of spacetime.[43]

---

[43] It is a remarkable fact that Plato's hero Timaeus expresses the following conviction: "Time, then, and the heaven came into being at the same instant in order that, having been created together, if ever there was to be a dissolution of them, they might be dissolved together." Plato, Timaeus 38 b.

B THE ARROW OF TIME AND IRREVERSIBLE PROCESSES

When considering the answer to the question whether the arrow of time affects the possibility of (mostly backward) time travels in section 9.3, I mentioned that I envisage a short consideration of the ontological status of the arrow of time, as well as a presentation of a part of Mellor's reasoning concerning the relation between observed irreversible processes and the arrow of time in *Appendix B*.

Let me begin with the arrow of time. As I showed in section 4.4, the asymmetry of time is manifested by what is often referred to by the expression "arrows of time". In fact, I had in mind three arrows – the thermodynamic, the cosmological, and the psychological one. But in so far as they have one and the same direction, I can speak here generally about *the* arrow of time. I come back to this topic, because I want to clear one tacitly shared misunderstanding – that of connecting the arrow of time with the flow of time. Of course, for those who believe that the flow of time is not mind-dependent, but is a real physical process, this connection is self-evident: the arrow of time simply shows the direction of the time flux – from the past, through the present and to the future. But authors like me, who accept the flow of time to be mind-dependent, give some different meaning to the arrow of time. It is precisely presented by Paul Davies:

> Many people muddle the flow of time with the arrow of time. This is understandable, given the metaphor. Arrows, after all, fly – as time is supposed to. But arrows are also employed as static pointers, such as a compass to indicate north, or a weather vane to show

the direction of the wind. It is in the latter sense that arrows are used in connection with time... I discussed the fumbling attempts by physicists to pin down the arrow of time. The quality this arrow describes is not the *flux* of time, but the asymmetry or lopsidedness of the physical world *in* time, the distinction between past and future directions of time.

Time does not have to *flow* from past to future for a time asymmetry to be manifested. (Davies 1995: 256-257, his italics)

So, the arrow of time, as I and authors like Paul Davies understand it, does not indicate a flow of time, but the direction in which the physical world is "lopsided".

Now we come to the place where the irreversible processes are invited for the sake of giving meaning to their relation to the arrow of time. Very often philosophers and scientists are inclined to declare that it is just because of the irreversible processes in nature that time displays its asymmetry. In section 4.4 I have already tried, though in a succinct way, to elucidate the relation between observed irreversible processes and the arrow of time, while supporting the opposite view. I contend that the irreversible processes do not determine the arrow of time, but it is the opposite way – the arrow of time underlies the irreversible processes. The reason is that they are nomologically contingent, i.e. they depend on specific initial and boundary conditions, which, if being settled otherwise, this would alter their course.

Let us take for example a well-known class of irreversible processes – that of wave radiation. The irreversibility of these processes is expressed by the following statement: "Radiation expands outwards from its source". But can we never see the opposite spreading of waves, from a distant place to the source?

Imagine a round pool full of water and a stone falling at its center. It would certainly produce circle waves spreading away from the point where it fell. Imagine also an appropriately constructed fence going around along the edge of the pool. The fence would reflect then the water waves back to their source – the place where the stone has fallen. So we can become witnesses of a backward radiation. But this does not mean that something happens to the arrow of time!

D. H. Mellor (1998: 120) raises the following claim, which I shall call Mellor's thesis (MT):

(MT) "Irreversibility has nothing to do with what gives time its direction. The fact is that the direction of time does not depend on the existence of irreversible processes."

In order to provide an argument for this claim Mellor adduces a simple example that I find to be quite convincing, and to this effect it deserves to be presented here in short.

Let us have a look at three different types of clocks (Mellor 1998: 120-121). Clock c is an ordinary clock the big hand of which moves from the indication 12, then past that of 1, of 2, and so on. The hand moves in one and the same clockwise direction and follows one and the same causal order when passing through the different hour indications. Let us also imagine a clock c', that gives an account of time, but which is travelling back in time. In other words, c' is also a clockwise clock. In the end let us imagine a third clock c'', the hands of which are *constructed* to move anti-clockwise. Now let us suppose that the hand of clock c becomes bent at its edge just when it is reaching 1. Then it will remain bent when moving toward indication 2, 3, and so on, since the change in the hand is an irreversible process (Mellor 1998: 121).

If this is the real state of affairs, what is the case with clock c', travelling back in time? We shall see the same picture as of clock c, merely because of the unchanged causal order producing the irreversible bending of the clock's hand. However, the hand of clock c'' will manifest a different behavior, since the causal order is changed due to its anti-clockwise movement.

This thought experiment clearly demonstrates that we can register different courses of an irreversible process, while the arrow of time stays the same. Thus (MT) receives a good illustration.

But an answer to a relevant question still remains unclear. The question is "Are all irreversible processes nomologically contingent?"

If the answer is positive, then the validity of (MT) stays intact. But what if the answer is negative? This would mean that there is at least one irreversible process which is nomological. If so, then we face the following dilemma: we must either conclude that (MT) is false, or that the process in question is not "an ordinary" irreversible process, but is another manifestation of the arrow of time, i.e. of the asymmetry of time itself.

In the middle of the previous century quantum physicists came upon such a process that looked quite unexpected for them – *the asymmetry in time* between the creation and the decay of a sub-atomic particle. This newly discovered particle is the neutral K-meson, or kaon for short.

> A typical kaon is produced by the strong force, in a trice, following the collision of two strongly interacting nuclear particles. However, although the kaon decays into other strongly interacting particles (pions), it takes as long as a nanosecond to do so. This came as a shock. If a particle can be made in a trillion-trillionth of a second by a particular sort of process, why doesn't the particle decay in about the same time by the same sort of process? What goes forwards should go backwards. The situation is rather like throwing a ball in the air and finding it takes a million years to come down again. What is it that leads the kaon to take trillions of times longer to decay than it takes to be produced?

> At stake here was an almost sacred principle of physics that had been accepted without question for as long as anyone could remember – the principle of the reversibility of all fundamental physical processes. (Davies 1995: 209)

Today one can certainly say that "the principle of the reversibility of all fundamental physical processes" is not violated, since a kaon is produced by a strong interaction and decays under a weak interaction, which takes a longer time for its realization than the first process leading to the birth of a kaon. However, the decay of this particle is still accompanied by a strange behavior exhibiting a temporal asymmetry.

The "mechanism" of this strange situation concerning the kaon's decay has been revealed. It has turned out that the kaon exists as a mixture of two kinds of mesons, "oscillating" between both of them. The one is constructed by an anti-strange quark and a d-quark, and the other – by a strange quark and anti-d-quark. The weak force can change reversibly the d- into s-quark (strange quark) and anti-s- into anti-d-quark, but I need not enter into special details. What is important here is that the quantum mixture of the two oscillating mesons by which the kaon is being built could be either symmetric or not under space reflection. This explains why the kaon has two different decay schemes – it could be transformed either into two, or into three pions. However, a strange behavior of the kaon was registered concerning (although a rare) violation of the "three pions" decay scheme, when the kaon turned into two pions instead. But this is a violation of the so called CP-symmetry keeping a system invariant under the change between a partical with an anti-particle accompanied with a mirror reflection of the system. But the violation of the CP-symmetry is equivalent to a *time asymmetry*.

> The humble kaon is able to tell the time in a limited sense: it knows the difference between the two *directions* of time, past and future. But in no way does the kaon *divide* time into past, present and future. (Davies 1995: 213, his italics)

All this means that the decay of the kaon into pions (pi-mesons) is not a usual irreversible process, but a process directly connected to and manifesting the time asymmetry. To this effect it is not an empirical threat to (MT).

Really, as I said, the mechanism of the strange situation concerning the kaon's decay has been revealed. But still discussions are going on concerning the reason for this curious fact; or in other words, concerning the reason why the natural world is not completely symmetrical, although it is very near to symmetry.

Let me remind my explanation to this problem presented in the end of section 4.4. I mentioned there the invariance of the quantum physical systems under a CPT-transformation. This means that they are invariant, i.e. they will stay the same, when subjected to three simultaneous transformations: changing the elementary particles with their respective anti-particles (which would change their electric charges with the opposite ones), indicated by "C", a mirror transformation of the system, indicated by "P", and changing the sign of the time variable, indicated by "T". If one of these transformations is not applied, the system could prove not to stay invariant.

But why the physical world is not always invariant in relation to only one of these transformations, or to the different couples of them? As it seems a possible answer to this question could refer to some fundamental quality of our universe.

In the early stage of the evolution of the universe elementary particles and anti-particles were born, but later the material structures of our visible universe were made only by particles, and not by anti-particles. This means that the CP-symmetry in the early universe proves to be broken, although in a very small scale: after a vehement annihilation among one billion particles and the same number of respective anti-particles, one particle managed to remain. Matter has overcome anti-matter. The decay of "the humble kaon" is a "reminiscence" of this asymmetry.

In my view, this asymmetry, which has given birth to a universe with material (and not anti-material) planets, stars, galaxies and huge galactic configurations, was compensated by an additional asymmetry – that of time, so that the CPT-symmetry to be valid. Thus time obtained an arrow pointing the direction of the universal expansion. If I may say so, the "price" for the material universe is the arrow of time, or as Paul Davies (1995: 213) has put it, is that our universe is "lopsided".

This lopsidedness, as well as the breaking of the mirror symmetry in the quantum world, are not so strong, so that the universe to be almost symmetrical, and not so weak, so that the universe to be not empty of matter having a propensity to evolve.

References

Allison, Henry E. 1976. "The Non-Spatiality of Things in Themselves for Kant." *Journal of the History of Philosophy*, **14**, N 3, 313-321. Quoted from hph.2008.0364.

Anastassov, Anastas. 1973. "On the Logical Structure of Physical Theories and Particularly of the Relativity Theory (Space, Time, Matter)" (In Bulgarian) In: *Contemporary Physics. Directions of Development, Methodological Problems*. Edited by A. Polikarov et al. Sofia: "Nauka I Izkustvo" , 241-262.

Arntzenius, Frank. 2012. *Space, Time and Stuff*. Oxford, New York: Oxford University Press.

Augustine, Saint, Bishop of Hippo. 1955. *Confessions and Enchiridion, newly translated and edited by Albert C. Outler*. Philadelphia: Westminster Press.

Baker, Lynne Rudder. 2010. "Temporal Reality." In: *Time and Identity. Topics in Contemporary Philosophy*. Edited by Joseph Keim Campbell, Michael O'Rourke, and Harry S. Silverstein. Cambridge, Massachusetts, London, England: The MIT Press.

Banham, Gary. 2009. "The Transcendental Aesthetic (2): Transcendental Idealism and Empirical Realism." In: *The Kant Course Lectures. Delivered at Manchester Metropolitan University 2009-2010*. http://www.garybanham.net/LECTURES.html

Bergson, Henri. 1911. *Creative Evolution*. New York: Henry Holt and Company.

Bonaccini, Juan Adolfo. 1998. "Concerninhg the Relationship between Non-Spatiotemporality and Unknowability of Things in Themselves in Kant's *Critique of Pure reason*." file:///D:/Neglected%20Alternative/Unknowability_NA.htm

Broad, C. D. 1923. *Scientific Thought*. London: Kegan Paul.

Callender, Craig. 2004. "There Is No Puzzle about the Low-Entropy Past." In: *Contemporary Debates in Philosophy of Science*. Edited by Christopher Hitchcock, Blackwell Publishing, 240-255.

Dainton, Barry. 2001. *Time and Space*. Acumen Publishing Limited.

Davies, Paul. 1990. *God and the New Physics*. Harmondsworth: Penguin Books.

Davies, Paul. 1995. *About Time. Einstein's Unfinished Revolution*. Harmondsworth: Penguin Books.

Einstein, Albert. (1936). "Physics and Reality." *J. F. I.*, March, 349-382. (Translation by Jean Piccard.) Hosted by Prof. M. Kostic at: www.costic.niu.edu

Empiricus, Sextus. 2007 (seventh printing). *Outlines of Scepticism*. Cambridge University Press.

Fearn, Nicholas. 2001. *Zeno and the Tortoise. How to Think like a Philosopher*. New York: Grove Press.

Greene. Brian. 2004. *The Fabric of the Cosmos: Space, Time, and the Texture of Reality*. New York: Vintage Books.

Greene. Brian. 2011. *The Hidden Reality. Parallel Universes and the Deep Laws of the Cosmos*. New York: Alfred A, Knopf, and Toronto: Random House of Canada Limited.

Hawking, Stephen. 1988. *A Brief History of Time*. Bantan Books.

Hawking, Stephen. 2001. *The Universe in a Nutshell*. London, New York, Toronto, Sydney, Auckland: Bantam Press.

Hawking, Stephen and Leonard Mlodinow. 2005. *A Briefer History of Time*. Bantam Press.

Hawking, Stephen and Leonard Mlodinow. 2010. *The Grand Design*. New York: Bantam Books.

Hegel, Georg Wilhelm Friedrich. 1892. *Lectures on the History of Philosophy*, Vol. I. Translated from the German by E. S. Haldane. London: Kegan Paul, Trench, Trübner & Co., LTD.

Hoerl, Christoph. 2008. "On Being Stuck in Time." *Phenomenology and the Cognitive Scinces*7 (4): 485–500.

Hoerl, Christoph. 2013. "Do We (Seem to) Perceive Passage?," *Philosophical Explorations: An International Journal for the Philosophy of Mind and Action*. doi:10.1080/13869795.2013.852615.

Hoerl, Christoph. 2014. „Time and the Domain of Consciousness." *Annals of the New York Academy of Sciences*, (1): 1-7.

Kant, Immanuel. 1998. *Critique of Pure Reason*. Translated by Paul Guyer and Allen W. Wood. Cambridge: Cambridge University Press.

Kroes, Peter. 1984. "Objective versus Minddependent Theories of Time Flow." *Synthese*, **61**, 423-446.

Mazzola, Claudio. 2014. "Does Time Flow, at any Rate?" *Metaphysica. International Journal for Ontology and Metaphysics*, 2014, DOI: 10.1515/mp-2014-0010, De Gruyter.

McTaggart, J. M. E. 1908. "The Unreality of Time." *Mind*, **17**,

457-474.

Miller, Kristie. 2013. "Presentism, Eternalism, and the Growing Block." In: *A Companion to the Philosophy of Time*. Edited by Heather Dyke and Adrian Bardon , John Wiley & Sons, Inc.

Miller, Kristie. 2018. "The cresting wave: a new moving spotlight theory." *Canadian Journal of Philosophy*, DOI: 10.1080/00455091.2018.1519770.

Minkowski, Hermann. 2012. *Space and Time. Minkowski's Papers on Relativity*. Edited by V. Petkov, Montreal: Minkowski Institute Press.

Mellor, D. H. 1998. *Real Time II*. London and New York: Routledge.

Mulder, Ruward A. and Dennis Dieks. 2016. "Determinism and Indeterminism on Closed Timelike Curves." In: *General Relativity 1916 – 2016*. Edited by Stefanov, Anguel S. and Marco Giovanelli, Montreal: Minkowski Institute Press.

Musser, George. 2017. "Spacetime Is Doomed." In: *Space, Time and the Limits of Human Understanding*. Edited by Wuppuluri, Shyam and Giancarlo Ghirardi, Springer, 217-227.

Paul, L. A. 2012. "Temporal Experience." In: *The Future of the Philosophy of Time*. Edited by A. Bardon, New York: Routledge, 99-122.

Penrose, Roger. 1989. *The Emperor's New Mind*. Oxford University Press.

Petkov, Vesselin. 2005. *Relativity and the Nature of Spacetime*. Berlin, Heidelberg: Springer.

Petkov, Vesselin. 2013. *From Illusions to Reality. Time, Spacetime and the Nature of Reality*. Montreal: Minkowski Institute Press.

Price, Hew. 2004. "On the Origin of the Arrow of Time: Why There Is Still a Puzzle about the Low-Entropy Past." In: *Contemporary Debates in Philosophy of Science*. Edited by Christopher Hitchcock, Blackwell Publishing, 219-239.

Prosser, Simon. 2000. "A New Problem for the A-Theory of Time." *The Philosophical Quarterly*, **50**, No. 201, 494-498.

Prosser, Simon. 2012. "Why Does Time Seem to Pass?" *Philosophy and Phenomenological Research*, **85** : 92–116.

Sagan, Carl. 1975. *The Cosmic Connection. An Extraterrestrial Perspective*. New York: Dell Publishing Co., Inc.

Sakon, Takeshi. 2016. "Time without Rate." *Philosophical Papers*, **45**, No. 3 (November 2016): 471-496.

Sayers, Sean. 1991. "Contradiction and Dialectic." *Science & Society*, **55**, No. 1.

Sider, Theodore. 2005. "Traveling in A- and B-Time." *The Monist*, **88**, No 3, 329–330.

Smith, Nicholas, J. J. 2011. "Inconsistency in the A-Theory." *Philosophical Studies*, **156**, 231-247.

Skow, Bradford. 2016. *Objective Becoming.* Oxford University Press.

Stefanov, Anguel. 2015. *Kant's Conceptions of Space and Time and Contemporary Science.* Montreal: Minkowski Institute Press.

Tooley, M. 1997. *Time, Tense and Causation.* Oxford: Oxford University Press.

Varzi, A. 2005. "Introduction." *The Monist*, **88**, N 3.